D1065220

A MAN
OF NO
IMPORTANCE

A MAN OF NO IMPORTANCE

A New Musical

Book by Terrence McNally
Music by Stephen Flaherty
Lyrics by Lynn Ahrens

Stage and Screen
New York

A Man of No Importance
Book by Terrence McNally
Music by Stephen Flaherty
Lyrics by Lynn Ahrens
Based on the motion picture produced by Little Bird
Stage & Screen edition copyright © 2003 by Terrence McNally and Lynn Ahrens
Libretto Copyright © 2003 by Terrence McNally
Music Copyright © 2003 by Stephen Flaherty
Lyrics Copyright © 2003 by Lynn Ahrens
All rights reserved

Photos by Paul Kolnik

Inquiries concerning stock and amateur rights should be addressed to Music Theatre International (MTI), 421 W. 54th St., New York, NY 10019. 212-541-4684. http:www.mtishows.com

Original cast album available on Jay Records. Vocal selections for "A Man of No Importance" are published by Warner Chappell Music.

ISBN: 1-58288-044-1

Printed in the United States of America

The glory of the theatre is also its bane: you have to be there to experience it. When a production closes, it is gone forever. It lives in the memory of a lucky few and when they are gone, it disappears with them. There are published scripts, of course, and original cast recordings but they only tell part of the story.

I wouldn't have it any other way. Life itself is ephemeral and theatre is the art most like life as I have so far experienced it: transitory, unpredictable, overwhelming, and finally, quite wonderful.

No wonder making theatre is like catching at moonbeams. In every project there comes a time when it seems quite impossible. And yet we do it, generation after generation, no matter the risks and the possibilities for failure. Theatre is a deep reflection of the human community.

A Man of No Importance is about a group of theatrical amateurs who dedicate the off hours in their routine lives to catching at some of those moonbeams. In their "real" lives they work hard for their money. In their "true" lives they work even harder to make art for their audience of friends and family.

In so doing, they become People of Great Importance, but most of all their leader, Alfie Byrne, a Dublin bus conductor, who learns in the course of tumultuous rehearsals for his long-dreamed-of production of Oscar Wilde's *Salome* that the theatre is not a place to hide from the world but instead the very place where we may finally discover our true selves. The defeat of his production is also the victory of his self. The small world of the St. Imelda's Players becomes an enormous one and I would be surprised if you did not find at least a small part of your world in theirs. Alfie and his friends are all of us.

Man was a charmed show from its inception through its writing, and a happy experience to rehearse. Our musical, of course, is based on a film of the same name. I am always indebted to Simon Beaufoy, who wrote the original screenplay. I am equally indebted to Lincoln Center Theatre where the production was developed with integrity and compassion, a rare combination in the *mondo agitato* of New York theatre. Joe Mantello, our director, gave us a cast and production that could not be bettered.

My greatest debt, however, is to my collaborators, Lynn Ahrens and Stephen Flaherty, for writing words and music that do not condescend to these ordinary people but instead discover the poetry and yes, even the greatness in them.

A Man of No Importance indeed!

And although this published text is only part of our story, it is a crucial one. As you read it, imagine another rainy morning on the streets of Dublin. A man is heading off to work. His sister straightens his tie. Imagination is not the same thing as a theatre ticket stub but it has its own rewards as well.

—Terrence McNally
January 19, 2003

PRODUCTION HISTORY

A Man of No Importance opened October 10, 2002, at Lincoln Center Theatre at the Mitzi E. Newhouse under the direction of Andre Bishop and Bernard Gersten. It was directed by Joe Mantello. Set design was by Loy Arcenas, costume design by Jane Greenwood, lighting design by Donald Holder, and sound design by Scott Lehrer. Music direction was by Ted Sperling, vocal arrangements by Stephen Flaherty; the conductor was Rob Berman and orchestrations were by William David Brohn & Christopher Jahnke. Casting was by Tara Rubin Casting, the stage manager was Michael Brunner, the musical theatre associate producer was Ira Weitzman, general manager was Adam Siegel, production manager was Jeff Hamlin, the director of marketing & special projects was Thomas Cott and the director of development was Hattie K. Jutagir. Musical staging was by Jonathan Butterell. The assistant stage manager was Janet Takami.

THE CAST
(in order of appearance)

Alfie Byrne	Roger Rees
Father Kenny	Jarlath Conroy
Mrs. Grace/Kitty Farrelly	Katherine McGrath
Miss Crowe	Barbara Marineau
Mrs. Curtin	Patti Perkins
Baldy O'Shea	Ronn Carroll
Rasher Flynn/Carson	Michael McCormick
Ernie Lally	Martin Moran
Mrs. Patrick	Jessica Molaskey
Sully O'Hara	Sean McCourt
Peter/Breton Beret	Luther Creek
Lily Byrne	Faith Prince
Carney/Oscar Wilde	Charles Keating
Robbie Fay	Steven Pasquale
Adele Rice	Sally Murphy

UNDERSTUDIES
For Alfie Byrne, Ernie Lally - James Hindman;
for Father Kenny, Baldy O'Shea, Rasher Flynn/Carson - Sean McCourt;
for Mrs. Grace/Kitty Farrelly, Miss Crowe, Mrs. Curtin, Lily Byrne - Barbara Tirrell;
for Sully O'Hara, Peter/Breton Beret, Robbie Faye - Wayne Wilcox;
for Mrs. Patrick, Adele Rice - Michelle Federer;
for Carney/Oscar Wilde - Michael McCormick

SETTING AND CHARACTERS

TIME
1964

PLACE
Dublin, Ireland

THE CHARACTERS

ALFIE BYRNE. A middle-aged Dublin bus driver and amateur theatre director.

FATHER KENNY. A priest.

MRS. GRACE. A housewife. (Doubles as Kitty Farrelly, a barmaid.)

MISS CROWE. A spinster.

MRS. CURTIN. Mother of nine.

BALDY O'SHEA. A widower.

RASHER FLYNN. A heavy smoker and ex-All-Ireland gymnast. (Also doubles as Carson, an inspector for the Dublin Bus Company.)

ERNIE LALLY. An accountant.

MRS. PATRICK. A member of the Sodality.

SULLY O'HARA. Unemployed.

BRETON BERET. A young no-account at the pub. (Also doubles as Peter, the lad who sweeps up the church hall.)

LILY BYRNE. Alfie Byrne's middle-aged, unmarried sister.

CARNEY. A butcher with thespian aspirations. (Also doubles as Oscar Wilde.)

ROBBIE FAY. Alfie's young partner on the bus.

ADELE RICE. A young, unmarried woman.

A MAN
OF NO
IMPORTANCE

 **ACT I**

AT RISE: The Social Hall adjacent to St. Imelda's, a small parish church in a quiet neighborhood of Dublin.

It is 1964. It is spring. The room, a large one, is dark now but a little sunlight manages to filter through the windows which are both dirty and made of an opaque-ish glass.

Though we cannot see into the room very clearly, we are very aware of the sound of a flute playing a somewhat melancholy air. We bask in it a moment. It's a beautiful tune.

This continues a short while, even as we hear sounds from outside. The door is opened and a little more sunlight comes into the hall.

A man has come into the room. His name is ALFIE BYRNE. *He is in his 40s, average looks and build. He wears a Dublin bus conductor's uniform, cap and ticket-dispensing gear.*

He does not turn on the lights at first, but stands there, silhouetted against the door.

ALFIE BYRNE:

"How beautiful is the Princess Salome tonight! She is like the shadow of a white rose in a mirror of silver. She is like a dove that has strayed. She is like a narcissus trembling in the wind. She is like a silver flower."

FATHER KENNY:

(*off*) Who's there? Is somebody in there?

(ALFIE *ignores this. He doesn't even seem to hear it. The flute music continues*)

ALFIE: "You are always looking at her. You look at her too much. It is dangerous to look at people in such a fashion. Something terrible may happen."

FR. KENNY:
    Would that be you in there, Alfie Byrne?

ALFIE: "Ah! I have kissed thy mouth, Jokanaan, I have kissed thy mouth. There was a bitter taste but what matter? What matter? I have kissed thy mouth."

(*We see another man's figure come into the room. He quickly turns on the overhead lights and we see that we are in a large church hall with scattered chairs and tables in general disarray. Most importantly, there is a small stage at one end of the hall for amateur theatricals. The shabby red curtain is closed.*)

FR. KENNY:
    Standing here in the dark like a ghost! You should be outside. It's the first sun we've had all spring.

ALFIE: Being Ireland, it's probably the last. Have you come to gloat, too, Father? Watch the wretched man gather up his paper crowns and cardboard sandals?

FR. KENNY:
    Nobody's gloating, Alfie. I know how much this place meant to you.

ALFIE: No, you don't, Father.

FR. KENNY:
    I went to the Archbishop myself. "Surely," I told him, "There's another punishment to fit the crime."

ALFIE: Spare me your Gilbert and Sullivan, man!

FR. KENNY:

"Don't put him out," I said. "That little theatre is a holy place to Alfie Byrne. He loves St. Imelda's the same way some men love women."

ALFIE: I'm sure he had a fine smirk on him when he heard that one.

FR. KENNY:

The truth be told: you brought this on yourself, Alfie, no one else did. You should have told me this *Salome* was a dirty play.

ALFIE: It's not. It's art, Father, art!

FR. KENNY:

Why don't you leave this for later, and come to the cine with me?

ALFIE: A movie's cold comfort for a man who's lost his theatre. "Blessed are the poor of imagination, for they shall inherit the cinemas."

FR. KENNY:

It's not the end of the world, you know.

ALFIE: It's the end of mine, Father.

FR. KENNY:

I hope you won't take this the wrong way, Alfie, but the Abbey Theatre, St. Imelda's Players were not. Hell, you weren't even the Gate. You were bloody awful.

ALFIE: You may be right but we had a grand time thinking we were bloody wonderful. Didn't you ever want to go on the stage, Father?

FR. KENNY:
I do, every Sunday, it's called High Mass. Are you coming or not?

ALFIE: Ging's Theatricals will be wanting Herodias's crown back before closing time or it's another week's rent.

FR. KENNY:
I'll see you in confession.

ALFIE: No you won't, Father.

FR. KENNY:
Kindly pull the door when you go.

(FATHER KENNY *goes*)

ALFIE: WELL, I'LL SEE YOU, ST. IMELDA'S.
WHAT IS THERE TO SAY?
PULL THE DOOR AND PACK UP
THE CART.
WILL YOU MISS US, ST. IMELDA'S?
MISS OUR LITTLE PLAY?
MISS OUR SMALL PRETENSIONS
TO ART?

(*He begins to look through some remaining props*)

ALFIE: AH, BUT WHAT WE HAD WAS SOMETHING.
WHAT WE HAD WAS RARE.
NO ONE WOULD DENY IT WAS GRAND
ONCE THEY STOOD ON THIS STAGE
WITH A PROP IN THEIR HAND ...

(*During this we are aware of the red stage curtains stirring behind him.* ALFIE *is not.*

The curtains slowly part.

What is revealed—in a striking tableau—are the St. Imelda's Players.

The costumes are tacky, the lighting is crude but there is a spirit of innocence and simplicity, theatre at its most basic level.)

ALFIE: MRS. GRACE'S FAN
WHEN SHE PLAYED LADY BRACKNELL

MRS. GRACE:
    "Mr. Worthing! Rise, sir, from this semi-recumbent posture."

ALFIE: MISS CROWE'S DIADEM.

MISS CROWE:
    "Oh, Hamlet, thou has cleft my heart in twain."

ALFIE: MRS. CURTIN'S PARASOL.

MRS. CURTIN:
    (*Struggling to open it*) Damnit, you're supposed to open! Props!

ALFIE: ERNIE LALLY'S COAT.
RASHER FLYNN'S OLD HAT.

BALDY: Can we get started? Curtain going up!

(*The actors have begun to arrange the chairs in the hall into two rows with an aisle in the middle. They will soon become* ALFIE's *bus.*)

ALFIE: What are you doing, Baldy?

BALDY: We're putting on our own play.

RASHER: It's about time, too.

MISS CROWE:
           And you're the leading man this time. No standing out
           front telling us where to go and how to speak and when to
           pick up a prop.

MRS. CURTIN:
           We get to be ourselves this time. So do you.

MRS. GRACE:
           You need a little powder, luv, your brow is shiny. (*She pow-
           ders* ALFIE *vigorously*) Stand still!

ALFIE: I don't believe I know this play, Mrs. Grace.

MRS. GRACE:
           You will, Mr. Byrne.

ERNIE: We're all in it, taking all the parts.

RASHER: What are we gonna call it?

MRS. CURTIN:
           The Tragedy of Alfie Byrne, A Dublin Coachman or *A Man
           of No Importance.*

ERNIE: I think you mean *The Comedy of Alfie Byrne.*

BALDY: Beginners to the stage, on the double, curtain going up.
           Cue the rain. I said, cue the rain! Break a leg, Mr. Byrne.

(*Our play has begun!*)

"A MAN OF NO IMPORTANCE"

TROUPE MEMBERS:
IT'S A RAINY DUBLIN MORNING.
SKY A LEADEN GRAY.
BLACK UMBRELLAS PASSING.
JUST YOUR NORMAL DAY.

LILY: A WOMAN IS SLIDING TWO EGGS ON A PLATE,
CALLING HER BROTHER:
"NOW ALFIE,
YOU'RE LATE!"

TROUPE MEMBERS:
AND A MAN
IS BRUSHING THE LINT FROM HIS VEST.
JUST A MAN
HIS UNIFORM DUTIFULLY PRESSED.
NOW THE MAN
REMEMBERS A POEM THAT MAKES HIS HEART
YEARN . . .

LILY: BUT HIS SISTER SAYS
"STRAIGHTEN YOUR TIE!"

CARNEY: AND THE BUTCHER NEXT DOOR WAVES GOODBYE

ALL (BUT ALFIE):
TO A MAN OF NO IMPORTANCE

(*We hear the bell of a Dublin bus as* ROBBIE FAY *takes his place in the driver's seat*)

ROBBIE FAY:

      ENTER ROBBIE FAY.
      DRIVER OF THE BUS.
      JUST ANOTHER DAY
      FOR THE TWO OF US.

ALFIE: Me darlin' Bosie.

ROBBIE: Don't start! I got a head on me. We were playing snooker till all hours.

(He is already combing his hair in the bus mirror)

ALFIE: Golden hair, glinting in the winter sun.

ROBBIE: It's raining, it's March, me hair's not golden and me name's not Bosie. It's Robbie, I'll thank you very much.

(Starts the bus motor)

ALFIE: Drive on, fair Apollo. Race your engines, oh rare Athenian youth.

ROBBIE: So what are you giving them this morning?

ALFIE: Well, I propose to give them a treat today. They may choose any piece they like from my repertoire.

ROBBIE: I got a request for you. Do us that one, you know, "The dead are dancing with the dead."

ALFIE: You like that one, do you?

ROBBIE: I do, indeed.

ALFIE: That's my poet!

ROBBIE: Bollocks!

(*During this section, the other* ACTORS *sit down in the chairs, taking their customary places on the bus as* ALFIE *goes among them, collecting fares*)

TROUPE MEMBERS:
NOW THE MAN
GREETS PASSENGERS BOARDING THE BUS
AND THE BUS
BECOMES SOMETHING MORE THAN A BUS
AS THE MAN
TAKES TICKETS AND GIVES THEM
A VERSE IN RETURN . . .

ALL: AND A FEW SIMPLE HEARTS ARE THUS WARMED
AS A GRAY DUBLIN DAY IS TRANSFORMED
BY A MAN OF NO IMPORTANCE . . .

ALFIE: WHAT WE HAD WAS SOMETHING.
WHAT WE HAD WAS RARE.
POETRY AND ART IN THE AIR.
AND FRIENDS . . .

Good morning, my dear friends.

ALL: Good morning, Mr. Byrne.

ALFIE: With your permission, I will begin today's reading with "The Harlot's House" by Dublin's own immortal Oscar Wilde. That is, if you won't be telling the Sodality, Mrs. Patrick.

MRS. PATRICK:
My lips are sealed, Mr. Byrne.

ALFIE: It was requested by our very own coachman, Mr. Robbie
           Fay.

MRS. PATRICK:
           You should be ashamed of yourself, Robbie Fay.

(*He opens a small book of poetry and begins to read. The others listen intently. This is their favorite part of their day.*)

ALFIE: "We caught the tread of dancing feet,
           We loitered down the moonlit street,
           And stopped beneath the harlot's house."

ALL BUT ALFIE:
           PICTURE THE BUS
           AS IT MOVES DOWN A STREET
           PAST A WINDOW OF FISH
           AND A PRIEST ON A BIKE.
           A HANDFUL OF PEOPLE
           WITH JOURNEYS TO MAKE
           LEAVING THE EVERYDAY
           WORLD IN THEIR WAKE ...
           THEN IT'S BREAK.

(*The bus empties of its passengers.* ALFIE *takes out a brown paper
bag and offers* ROBBIE *a sandwich and a Guinness.*)

ROBBIE: ONE LITTLE GUINNESS.
           IT'S ALWAYS THE SAME.

ALFIE: A Guinness a day keeps the doctor away.

ROBBIE: You sound like my old man.

           SAFE AND SOUND,
           THAT'S THE NAME OF YOUR GAME.

ALFIE: It's good for you. Build up your muscles.

ROBBIE: It hasn't done much for you.

> THERE'S GOT TO BE MORE TO LIFE
> THAN ONE PINT OR THE POPE!
> TOO LATE FOR MY DA,
> BUT FOR YOU, MATE, THERE'S HOPE!
> AND WHAT KIND OF SANDWICH IS THIS?

ALFIE: Cucumber.

ROBBIE: Cucumber?

ALFIE: An ordinary sandwich immortalized in *The Importance of Being Earnest* at the Theatre Royal, Haymarket, on February 14, 1895—a night the mundane became sublime. That was a first performance, my friend.

ROBBIE: Were you there? I'm kidding. How old are you anyway?

ALFIE: Old enough to know a gentleman doesn't ask another gentleman that question.

ROBBIE: I'm not a gentleman and I thought it was ladies you weren't supposed to ask.

ALFIE: Eat your cucumber sandwich.

ROBBIE: Not much substance.

ALFIE: Eat!

(He gets ready to read/recite another poem. It is clear this is one of their lunchtime rituals.)

ALFIE: "Symphony in Yellow" by Oscar Fingal O'Flahertie Wills Wilde.

ROBBIE: (*Making himself comfortable*) I'm listening.

ALFIE: "An omnibus across the bridge
             Crawls like a yellow butterfly,
             And, here and there, a passers-by
             Shows like a little restless midge."

ROBBIE: "Midge!" "Midge" is good, I like midge. You don't have to
             know what it means to know what it means, you know
             what I mean, Alf?

ALFIE: That's because we feel poetry here, in our hearts. That's bet-
             ter than understanding with our minds. You're learning,
             that's good, you're learning.

          (CARSON, *their supervisor, discovers them*)

CARSON: What's going on here?

ALFIE: Damn, it's Carson! (*They quickly get the bus moving again*)
             You look like you could use a Guinness, Mr. Carson!

CARSON: You're eight minutes behind schedule! The Dublin Transit
             System doesn't take this laxness lightly. I'm warning you
             Byrne.

ALL BUT ALFIE:
             PICTURE THE BUS
             AS IT MOVES DOWN A STREET
             PAST A NUN WITH A SACK
             AND A BOY WITH A DOG.
             A BUS IN THE RAIN
             AND THE HUMBLEST OF MEN
             BRINGING HIS PASSENGERS
             HOME ONCE AGAIN . . .

ALFIE: Good afternoon, my dear friends.

ALL: Good afternoon, Mr. Byrne.

ALFIE: With your permission, I will continue with "The Harlot's
            House." (*He reads*)
            "Then turning to my love I said
            The dead are dancing with the dead.
            The dust is whirling with the dust.
            But she, she heard the violin,
            And left my side, and entered in;
            Love passed into the house of Lust."

ADELE RICE:
                A BLUE-COATED GIRL
                NO ONE'S NOTICED BEFORE
                ENTERS THE BUS,
                TAKES A SEAT BY THE DOOR . . .

    (*All eyes are on the newcomer*)

ALFIE: My friends, we have a new face. Permit me on your behalf
            to welcome her into our little circle. Welcome, my dear,
            welcome. Miss?

ADELE: Rice.

ALFIE: Miss Rice. Miss Rice's entrance matches perfectly the lines
            of our poem, our little rhyme.
            "Then suddenly the tune went false.
            The dancers wearied of the waltz.
            The shadows ceased to wheel and whirl.
            And down the long and silent street,
            The dawn with silver sandaled feet,
            Crept like a frightened girl."

    (*He puts his hand to his heart. The passengers applaud.*)

ERNIE: Fair play to you, Mr. Byrne, fair play!

ALL BUT ALFIE:
> JUST A MAN
> CONDUCTING HIS BUS THROUGH THE DAY
> BUT THE DAY IS NOW SOMETHING MORE THAN A
>   DAY
> AS THE MAN TAKES TICKETS
> AND LOOKS AT THE GIRL DRESSED IN BLUE.

ROBBIE: THEN HIS DRIVER YELLS,

> Alf, you okay?

ALL BUT ALFIE:
> AND THE BUS LUMBERS OFF ON ITS WAY

(*The passengers begin to exit again*)

GROUP 1:
> AS A MAN OF NO
> IMPORTANCE

GROUP 2:
> A MAN OF NO
> IMPORTANCE

GROUP 1:
> A MAN OF NO
> IMPORTANCE ...

GROUP 2:
> A MAN OF NO
> IMPORTANCE

ALL BUT ALFIE:
> A MAN OF NO IMPORTANCE
> ENDS HIS DAY ...

(*The bus is empty again. It's the end of their day.* ALFIE *puts his feet up.*)

ALFIE: Home, James. Take the scenic route. Through Phoenix Park, past Parliament House and straight on to Dreamland.

ROBBIE: YOU AND YOUR FANCIES.
THEY'RE ALWAYS A GRIN.

I wish I had your imagination, mate.

ALFIE: You do. You just don't use it.

(*They "arrive" at their terminal garage*)

ROBBIE: I'LL BET YOU FANCY
THAT GIRL WHO GOT IN.

ALFIE: Never mind the girl. And I've done the report.

ROBBIE: FOR A FELLA WHO'S GOT HIS HEAD
IN THE CLOUDS SUCH AS YOU,
YOU'RE DAMN FINE TO WORK WITH
AND I'M GLAD I DO.

ALFIE: Thanks Robbie. I like you, too.

ROBBIE: I'M OFF TO THE PUB THEN.

ALFIE: GOOD LUCK AT THE SNOOKER.

ROBBIE: DON'T WALK INTO WALLS, ALF.
THAT GIRL IS A LOOKER.

ALFIE: I'LL SEE YOU TOMORROW.

BOTH: AT SEVEN.

(ROBBIE *goes*)

ALFIE: IT'S A RAINY DUBLIN EVENING.
LAMPS ARE GOING ON.
BLACK UMBRELLAS PASSING,

PEOPLE COME AND GONE.
A UNIFORMED MAN
HURRIES HOME THROUGH THE NIGHT—
THREE BLOCKS DOWN COLLINS,
A LEFT, THEN A RIGHT.
AND NOTHING IS DIFFERENT
SAVE ONE RAY OF LIGHT
FOR A MAN OF NO IMPORTANCE.

(ALFIE *wends his lonely way home*)

TRANSITION

LILY AND ALFIE'S APARTMENT

(*We are in the small apartment* LILY *and* ALFIE *share next door to Mr. Carney's butcher shop*)

LILY: Alfie, who are you cooking for? The Queen of England? What's the occasion, anyway?

ALFIE: (*off*) Close your eyes! Are they closed?

LILY: Hurry up, will you? I'm starving!

(*She sits at table as* ALFIE *enters with a steaming bowl of food for them*)

ALFIE: *Eccola, mia sorella. Aprite gli occhi.* Open your eyes, Lil.

(LILY *eyes the bowl suspiciously*)

LILY: Merciful hour! I couldn't eat that.

ALFIE: You had it before, you liked it. It's spaghetti—with a Bolognese sauce

LILY: It's not curry, is it?

ALFIE: Curry's Indian, the fellas with the turbans.

LILY: Never eating curry again, not after the last time.

ALFIE: This is Italian.

LILY: Yeah, well, they're all darkies to me.

ALFIE: The Genoveses are Italian, Lily. The De Santees, the Volpes.
           They buy their vegetables off you.

LILY: Yeah, and look what they do with them. (*She toys miserably
           with her food*) Suppose I'll have to eat something to keep
           body and soul together. (*Suddenly*) All right, tell me. I know
           you're up to something. I'm not your sister for nothing,
           Alfie Fintan Byrne. I can read you like a book.

ALFIE: It's lucky for me you can't. (*He sits opposite. Then, confiden-
           tially.*) Remember this morning I said I—I had a feeling.

LILY: Oh, yeah, one of your premonitions.

ALFIE: Well, I was right. Someone I was waiting for, praying for
           even, got onto me bus out of the blue. A girl.

LILY: A girl! Oh, Alfie! Well, that is the power of the nine weeks
           of St. Jude for you! Excuse me while I faint. No, while I
           holler it out the window: Mum, Dad, wherever you are up
           there: tell Gabriel to blow his mighty horn. My own dear
           sweet little brother's in love!

"THE BURDEN OF LIFE"

LILY: HOW LONG HAS IT BEEN
          I'VE BEEN DOWN ON MY KNEES
          SAYING ROSARIES INTO MY SLEEP?

ALFIE: Lil!

LILY: THE CANDLES I'VE LIT!
          THE NOVENAS I'VE SAID
          IN THE HOPE ST. LAURETTA WOULD WEEP!

ALFIE: Lil!

LILY: THE GIRLS AT SODALITY
          CALL ME A MARTYR
          BUT THAT'LL BE ALL IN THE PAST
          NOW HEAVEN HAS LIFTED
          THE BURDEN OF LIFE
          AND HAS BROUGHT YOU A SWEETIE AT LAST!
          OH . . .
          YOU HAD BETTER PROPOSE TO HER FAST!

ALFIE: Are you through, Lily?

LILY: I'm all ears, Alf. Speak, lamb. Say sweet words to me, my
          only angel.

ALFIE: She's not for me. She's for me play.

LILY: Oh God, you're not starting that up again, are you? Wasn't
          last time enough for you?

ALFIE: If you're talking about *The Importance of Being Earnest!*

LILY: I'm talking about you making an utter fool of yourself.

ALFIE: A play like *Importance* needs more than a single performance to get it right. This time I intend to stage—for four performances—Oscar Wilde's masterpiece, *Salome*.

LILY: *Salome?* Is that out of the Bible?

ALFIE: It's nothing to do with the Bible or nine weeks on your knees to St. Jude. It's to do with art.

LILY: Art! Who puts these notions in your head? You're an unmarried bus conductor, Alfie, in case you haven't noticed.

I THINK OF THE TIMES
WE WAS BOTH OF US KIDS.
IT WAS ME WHO WOULD STAND UP FOR YOU.
I'D BEAT ANYBODY WHO'D
PICK ON MY BROTHER.
I'D PUMMEL 'EM PURPLE AND BLUE!
BUT, HERE I AM NOW, LOOKING AFTER YOU STILL!
THE GIRLS SAY I'M OUT OF MY HEAD,
AND PITY A WOMAN
THE BURDEN OF LIFE
WITH A BROTHER WHO'S NEVER BEEN WED.
OH, IT'S A BLESSING OUR PARENTS ARE DEAD!

ALFIE: Lil!

LILY: ST. LAURETTA
I DON'T EVEN MIND IF THE GIRL ISN'T VIRGINAL.
FAT CHANCE, THESE DAYS.
THERE'S PROBABLY THREE OF US
LEFT IN ALL IRELAND.

ST. LAURETTA
WITH ALL OF THE SCANDAL
YOU HEAR AND YOU READ OF TODAY,

OH, WHAT'S THE WHOLE WORLD COMING TO
ANYWAY?
AND NOW AND AGAIN, MR. CARNEY PROPOSES
AND ALL I CAN SAY IS—NOT YET.
MY BROTHER, HE NEEDS ME.
WHO ELSE HAS HE GOT
BUT SOME GIRL WHO HE STILL HASN'T MET!
AND NOW AND AGAIN I SEE GRAY IN YOUR HAIR
AND I NOTICE THE GRAY IN MINE, TOO.
OH, PITY A WOMAN THE BURDEN OF LIFE—
HOW MUCH MORE DO I HAVE TO GO THROUGH?

GOD SENT YOU THIS GIRL.
ALFIE GIVE IT A WHIRL
OR I'LL BASH IN YOUR BRAINS WITH MY SHOE!
ST. LAURETTA IS COUNTIN' ON YOU!

ALFIE: While you and St. Lauretta are up here planning my future,
           I'll just go downstairs and tell your Mr. Carney we're going
           up again.

LILY: Mr. Carney's as bad as you. You're both bewitched. There
           should be a law against it.

ALFIE :   What? The theatre?

LILY: No, your theatre, St. Imelda's. Well, while the two of you are
           going up, I'll be sitting down, watching Lucille Ball, a true
           talent, someone who is funny on purpose!

TRANSITION

CARNEY'S BUTCHER SHOP

(CARNEY *is waiting on a customer when* ALFIE *enters the shop*)

CUSTOMER:
    Tie it up good and tight, Mr. Carney.

CARNEY: No one trusses up a roast like William Carney.

ALFIE: Or lights up the stage at St. Imelda's either.

CARNEY: I try. I am the humble servant of the playwright, nothing less, nothing more.

ALFIE: We're going up.

CARNEY: We're what?

ALFIE: You heard me. We're going up again.

CARNEY: No!

ALFIE: First rehearsal early Monday evening. I promised Father Kenny we'd be out before the Bingo begins. Can I count on you?

CARNEY: You may indeed, sir. It's been too long entirely. I know we've had our differences—personal and artistic—but this time I will give you an Algernon for the ages.

CUSTOMER:
    What about my roast?

CARNEY: Take your bleeding roast.

CUSTOMER:
    It's not trussed properly.

ALFIE: The thing is that . . .

CUSTOMER:
I need a pound of your breakfast sausage.

CARNEY: We're closed, woman. Can't you see we're going up? (*To* ALFIE) You have made me the happiest of men. I'm what they call a creature of the theatre. Keep me off the stage too long and I start to shrivel up. My soul needs the exercise.

ALFIE: Have no fear, Mr. Carney. No matter what play we do, you're still my star.

CARNEY: God bless you, Alfie Byrne.

ALFIE: The ... er ... refreshments ...

CARNEY: Oh, no, no, don't worry. I will provide the ham for the rehearsal sandwiches. We'll let some of the others provide the ham for the performance.

ALFIE: Seven o'clock, Monday. St. Imelda's. You're the first to know. I'll go tell the others. Mr. Carney? He doesn't hear me.

(CARNEY *is already back on stage in a world of his own.* ALFIE *goes.*)

CARNEY: "The St. Imelda's Players have the distinct privilege of presenting for your play-going perusal and dramatic discernment *The Importance of Being Earnest* with Mr. William Carney in the leading role of Algernon. Mr. Carney, a familiar and beloved member of the St. Imelda's Players, is best known for his performances as Denny O'Connell, the irate father, in *A Night on the Town*, and Long John Silver in his own adaptation of *Treasure Island*, for which he also provided additional staging."

"GOING UP"

CARNEY: YOU'RE AT THAT DAILY GRIND
WHEN YOU SUDDENLY COME TO FIND
THAT YOU'RE GOING UP!

WHO GIVES A SAUSAGE THEN
FOR THE ORDERS OF MORTAL MEN
WHEN YOU'RE GOING UP!

WHEN LIFE'S ALL MEAGER SCRAPS,
DON'T YOU LOSE HEART, SIR.
DROP THAT CLEAVER,
GRAB THE OLD TAPS, AND PERHAPS

YOU'LL LAND A MEATY PART, SIR!
YOU BUTCHER, BUSMAN, CLERK!
THERE IS NO LINE OF WORK
THAT MAKES THE OLD MARROW GLOW
LIKE GOING UP!

(*Lights come up on* MRS. GRACE *at home*)

MRS. GRACE:
Margaret Grace returns to St. Imelda's after a brief absence brought on by her husband's condition. Maggie is perhaps best remembered for her Katisha in *The Mikado* and her portrayal of St. Joan. Her water colors may be seen in the lobby. They are for purchase.

(*Lights come up on* BALDY)

CARNEY: ONE MOMENT LIFE IS SLOW.

MRS. GRACE:
YOU'RE PAINTING PANSIES.

BALDY: FATE SHOWS UP
AND HANDS YOU A SHOW
AND HELLO!

ALL: YOU'RE GOING UP!

BALDY: James Michael O'Shea (or "Baldy" as he is known to one and all) has stage-managed every production at St. Imelda's since its founding. His late wife, Mary, will be remembered for her many performances on our stage. Mr. O'Shea is a retired publican.

   (*Lights come up on* MISS CROWE)

MISS CROWE:
     Oona Crowe was Miss Prism in last season's performance of *The Importance of Being Earnest* but her favorite role remains the title one in our centennial production of *Peter Pan.*

MISS CROWE, CARNEY, MRS. GRACE, BALDY:
     YOUR SKY IS PAINTED BLUE

MISS CROWE:
     YOU CAN FLY LIKE YOU'RE TWENTY-TWO

ALL: 'CAUSE YOU'RE GOING UP!

   (ERNIE *enters*)

ERNIE: Ernest Lally will be remembered by St. Imelda's audiences for his sterling portrayal of Mustard Seed in *A Midsummer Night's Dream.*

ALL PLUS ERNIE:
     YOU MAY PLAY ROYALTY

ERNIE:
>OR JUST SPEAR-BEARER NUMBER THREE

ALL FIVE:
>BUT YOU'RE GOING UP!

(RASHER *enters*)

RASHER: Rasher Flynn is a founding member of St. Imelda's and appeared in our inaugural production of *Pygmalion* as Colonel Pickering. In his youth, Rasher was an all-Ireland gymnast.

(*He takes a drag on his cigarette and coughs*)

SULLY O'HARA:
>Sully O'Hara, currently unemployed, is making his theatre debut with this production. Thank you.

ALL PLUS RASHER AND SULLY:
>THE HOUSE MAY NOT BE PACKED
>BUT DON'T LET GO, SIR.
>YOU'VE GOT SCENES TO PLAY!

CARNEY: (*Holding a piece of meat*) "Oh, that this too too solid flesh should melt."

ALL: YOU'VE GOT LINES TO SAY!

CARNEY: (*Holding a pig's head*) "Alas poor Yorick, I knew him Horatio!"

ALL: YOU'VE GOT FANS WHO WANT TO GET CARRIED AWAY!

(MRS. CURTIN *enters, dancing madly*)

MRS. CURTIN:
Maureen Curtin was a child star of the Dublin Music Hall and has kept her skills well-honed. This performance marks her return to the stage after some years. The Curtins have nine children: Deirdre, Padric, Rosaline, Fintan, Rebecca, Juliet, Anton, George Bernard, and Portia.

ALL:
THE HOUSE MAY NOT BE PACKED
BUT EVEN SO SIR . . .

CARNEY:
Bow to the highest ring. That's where you used to sit. Let them see your eyes, let them take you in, and then, with humility, the tip top of your head. You were good tonight, Carney. You're right, I was damn good!

ALL:
YOU BUTCHER, BUSMAN, CLERK!
THERE'S JUST ONE LINE OF WORK
THAT MAKES REAL LIFE
SEEM SO
LONG AGO
AND IT'S GOING UP!
GOING UP!
WE'RE GOING . . .

CARNEY:
Fellow thespians, prepare to meet your public.

ALL:
UP!

TRANSITION

THE BUS

(*The actors reassemble on the bus. They are waiting for* ALFIE *to tell them what their next production will be.*)

MISS CROWE:
What play are we doing, Mr. Byrne? Why are you keeping us in suspense?

BALDY: My vote is for *An Ideal Husband*.

MRS. GRACE:
We just did that one.

BALDY: You'll do it till you get it right.

ROBBIE: What are we waiting for, Alfie? We're already behind schedule. Carson will have a stroke.

ALFIE: Here she comes now.

(ADELE *hurries onto the bus*)

ADELE: I'm sorry, I was at the doctor's. Thank you for waiting.

(*She opens her purse.* ALFIE *puts up his hand.*)

ALFIE: A princess of Judea does not pay to ride a Dublin motor coach.

ADELE: I don't understand.

(CARSON, *the bus line supervisor, approaches, watch in hand*)

CARSON: Behind schedule you are again and it's not even noon. That's my last warning.

ALFIE: And good morning to you, Mr. Carson.

CARSON: Tickets, please. (*He stops in front of* ADELE) This woman has no ticket.

ALFIE: Why, I must have overlooked the young lady. There you are, miss.

(*He dispenses her a ticket from the machine*)

CARSON: The bus company is not a charity. If you want to provide free transport for wasters, that's up to you. But if I come on and find a tinker without a ticket, I'll put *you* off the bus— not them. Mark me now, Byrne.

(CARSON *exits*)

ALFIE: Good morning, my dear friends.

ALL: Good morning, Mr. Byrne

ALFIE: Our next production—and I will need your support, hard work and talent as never before—will be Oscar Wilde's masterpiece *The Tragedy of Salome, Princess of Judea.*

MRS. GRACE:
            That's the play with the immodest dancing in it, is it not, Mr. Byrne?

ALFIE: It is the play with the sublime Dance of the Seven Veils, Mrs. Grace. It is not immodest, it is art.

MRS. GRACE:
            Mr. Grace would never allow me to exhibit myself undulating in flimsy garments.

ALFIE: And for that we are grateful to Mr. Grace. We need your majestic talents to embody the role of Herodias, wife of Herod, mother of Salome.

MRS. GRACE:
            Does she dance?

ALFIE: Not a muscle.

MRS. GRACE:
            Thank God.

ALFIE: Exactly my sentiments, Mrs. Grace.

MRS. GRACE:
            Who's playing Herod? I have to know who my partner is.

BALDY: No one gives a rat's ass who's playing Herod when you're putting on *Salome*. If anyone on this bus is playing a sixteen-year-old virgin, I want to be first in line to buy a ticket for the comedy of the century.

ALFIE: "How beautiful is the Princess Salome tonight."

            (*He gets down on one knee in front of* ADELE)

ADELE: What are you all looking at?

ALFIE: "How pale the Princess is! Never have I seen her so pale. She is like the shadow of a white rose in a mirror of silver."

ADELE: I didn't move to Dublin to be made fun of! Go to hell, all of you, I'll walk.

ALFIE: Miss Rice!

ADELE: (*Whirling around*) I expected more from city folk, but I guess human nature is what it is, big city or village: mean spirited and vile. A single girl is the butt for anyone's jokes.

ALFIE: I meant no offense. That was my inappropriate way of asking you to be in our little play.

ADELE: Play? What play?

ALFIE: *Salome* by Oscar Wilde. She's a beautiful princess, like you Miss Rice.

ADELE: I'm not an actress.

ALFIE: We're an amateur group. We do it for fun, for love. We're all friends. You'd just be one of us. The moment I set eyes on you, Miss Rice, I knew I'd found my Salome.

ADELE: I'm too shy. I'd get the giggles or I'd faint.

ALFIE: No, you wouldn't. You'd be in another world entirely: a world of your creation.

ADELE: Who's my prince? You, I suppose.

ALFIE: Oh, no. Dear Lord, no. I'm no leading man, onstage or off. (*Taking her aside, so the others won't hear*) I'm hoping Robbie, my partner in crime on the bus, our driver, I'm hoping he'll play . . . well, Jokanaan's not really a prince, but you are in love with him.

ADELE: That wouldn't be too hard. He's a looker.

ALFIE: Yes, he is, and no, it wouldn't. What do you say?

"PRINCESS"

ADELE: HOW CAN A GIRL WHO'S FROM
A SOMEPLACE NORTH OF NOWHERE
BE A PRINCESS?
WHAT IN THE WORLD
WOULD MAKE YOU THINK THAT I WAS QUALIFIED
FOR PLAYING THE PART?

ALFIE: I have an instinct for talent.

ADELE: I'M FROM ROSCOMMON, WHERE
THE MAJOR ENTERTAINMENT
IS TO SIT OUTSIDE THE PUB
AND WATCH A FLY ON DOG SHITE—

I'm not joking!

THEY HAVE THEIR FOOTBALL AND THEIR BIBLES
AND THEY DON'T BELIEVE IN ART.

ALFIE: I'll help you. I'll take you through it line by line.

ADELE: HERE STANDS A SHOPGIRL WHO PUTS PRICES
ON THE PRODUCE,
NOT A PRINCESS.

MY ROYAL PALACE IS
THE BACK ROOM OF A BOARDINGHOUSE,
BRICK WALL FOR A VIEW.

I DON'T PRETEND TO BE A THING BUT
PLAIN AND COMMON.

WHEN YOU'RE BROUGHT UP IN ROSCOMMON,
WHAT'S THE USE PRETENDING?

I LEAVE THE FAIRYTALE ENDING
TO THE PEOPLE SUCH AS YOU.

ALFIE: Miss Rice . . .

ADELE: THEY DON'T RAISE DREAMERS IN ROSCOMMON,
ONLY ONIONS AND POTATOES.
YOU CAN ONLY TALK ABOUT POTATOES SO LONG.
NO ONE THERE COULD EVER SEE
WHAT YOU SEEM TO SEE IN ME . . .

ALFIE: WELL, POSSIBLY, ROSCOMMON
         WAS WRONG . . .

         It can be beautiful out there, playing a part, losing yourself in another person. Just for once, Miss Rice, being somebody new. I'm throwing myself at your feet, your royal highness.

ADELE: I DON'T SUPPOSE I'LL EVER
         HAVE ANOTHER CHANCE TO PLAY
         A PRINCESS.

         AND HERE IN DUBLIN IT APPEARS
         THAT THE PREVAILING MINDS
         ARE NOT QUITE SO SMALL.

         I SWORE I WOULDN'T SPEND MY LIFE
         BACK IN ROSCOMMON,
         I'D BE SOMEONE GOING SOMEPLACE
         THEY WOULD NEVER DREAM OF . . .

         THE ONLY DREAMER THAT ROSCOMMON
         WILL BE ABLE TO RECALL.

         SEEMS LIKE ROSCOMMON
         RAISED A PRINCESS AFTER ALL.

ALFIE: My friends, our Princess Salome.

TRANSITION

ST. IMELDA'S SOCIAL HALL

(ALFIE, BALDY, FATHER KENNY *and* PETER, *a young custodian at the hall who is arranging chairs*)

FR. KENNY:

> So you're trying it again this year? Your little drama group?

ALFIE: The muses of the theatre are calling, Father Kenny.

FR. KENNY:

> Do you think you will manage it this time?

ALFIE: We're quietly confident, Father.

FR. KENNY:

> And will it be the same play? You're not changing it are you?

ALFIE: No, it's another one. It's about John the Baptist.

FR. KENNY:

> John the Baptist. You'll need lots of water then, Mr. Byrne, a river Jordan, so to speak.

ALFIE: No water. His beheading. It's a very dry play we'll be doing, Father Kenny. No mopping up after us, Peter.

FR. KENNY:

> That's a relief. Water and bingo, that's not a good mix. But it's a biblical theme. That's a good thing, a fine thing. (MRS. PATRICK *enters*) Here's Mrs. Patrick with the keys. Wonderful woman. Don't know what the Sodality would do without her. She'd make you a fine wife.

MRS. PATRICK:

> I'm married, Father Kenny.

FR. KENNY:

> Ah, yes. All the good ones usually are.

ALFIE: Could I have the keys now, Father?

FR. KENNY:
John the Baptist—isn't there a dance in there somewhere? Would it be immodest dancing? The Archbishop is very strong on immodest dancing.

ALFIE: Not immodest, Father Kenny. It's art.

FR. KENNY:
Ah, art. Well, here are the keys. And you might drop up the script sometime.

ALFIE: We'll do that.

MRS. PATRICK:
The archbishop is very strong on a lot of things. It must be exhausting.

(FATHER KENNY *and* MRS. PATRICK *go.* PETER *gets a broom and begins to sweep.*)

ALFIE: We can't perform in a dark theatre, Baldy. Have you fixed the lights, yet?

BALDY: Unfortunately for you, I have. That's what was wrong with your last production: people could see it. Here goes nothing.

(*He throws the switch. The lights come on.*)

ALFIE: You're a genius! You are the rock on which the St. Imelda's Players are built.

BALDY: Don't tell Carney that! Does he know what play you're doing?

ALFIE: He doesn't care about the play. He only cares about the size of his part.

BALDY: He's in the Sodality of the Sacred Heart, remember.

ALFIE: Carney has a starring role, that will go a long way to molli-
            fy his Catholic principles. Give us a hand, will you, Peter?
            You still saving up your coppers to go to London and
            become the fifth Beatle?

PETER: I'm going to start my own band: The Annihilators. Irish
            music for Irishmen!

ALFIE: Art is for everyone, Peter. And if it's not, it should be.

PETER: Don't take this personal, Mr. Byrne, but art is for old fogies.
            Rock and roll is the future.

ALFIE: Lord, I hope you're wrong.

PETER: I'll get more chairs.

(He goes as they begin to set up chairs)

ALFIE: Ah, Baldy, as many times as I've done this, the first reading
            is still in some ways the most magic time of all in the the-
            atre. Our first encounter with the playwright's words. Our
            tongues fumbling with the poetry of his heart. No precon-
            ceptions. True creativity reigns.

"FIRST REHEARSAL"

ALFIE: THIS ROOM IS THE TETRARCH'S TERRACE.
            THAT LIGHTBULB, THE EVENING STAR!
            THOSE OLD LEATHER BOOTS YOU'RE WEARING—

BALDY: Roman sandals!

ALFIE: YES, THEY ARE!
           IN OUR EMPIRE VAST, A COOL NIGHT BREEZE
           IS BLOWING ACROSS THE SAND
           AND IN TWENTY SECONDS, AT THAT DOOR,
           THE EMPRESS HERSELF WILL STAND!

BOTH: OH, THE EMPRESS HERSELF WILL STAND!

   (*The St. Imelda's players are arriving*)

MRS. GRACE:
           "Give me my robe, put on my crown, I have immortal long-
           ings in me."

ALFIE: A wonderful reading, as usual, Mrs. Grace, but you're in the
           wrong play. (*He hands her a script*) Wonderful to have you
           back Mrs. Curtin.

MRS. CURTIN:
           When I left the house, the eight-year-old was strangling the
           four-year-old, the dishes were stacked to the ceiling and the
           old man was watching the telly with his trousers open. And
           people ask why I love the theatre.

   (*She takes her script*)

ALFIE: I HAVEN'T BEEN HALF SO HAPPY
           SINCE I DON'T REMEMBER WHEN.
           MY FRIENDS IN THE ROOM TOGETHER . . .

ALFIE AND MISS CROWE:
           WE'RE BACK ON THE BOARDS AGAIN!

ALFIE: Miss Crowe!

MISS CROWE:

> (*Inhaling mightily*) There's something about a theatre, even this one. You can almost smell it.

ALFIE: Especially this one.

(He hands her a script)

PETER: (*sweeping*) Coming through.

ALFIE: Gentlemen.

(He starts passing out scripts)

CARNEY: I just want someone to tell me why we're not doing *The Importance of Being Earnest* again.

BALDY: Because we found someone new. People are tired of looking at your old mug.

ALFIE: Mr. Carney, you are to play King Herod, a magnificent dramatic role. Quite a change for you, I think you'll find it.

CARNEY: I like a challenge. Mind you, I like a big part, as well.

(ADELE is the last to arrive)

ADELE: Is this the right place?

ALFIE: Here's our Princess Salome. Welcome to our little theatre, Miss Rice. We're about to begin.

(Polite applause for ADELE. The men are more enthusiastic than the women.)

ALFIE: As for our Jokanaan, our John the Baptist, the young man
            I have in mind has not yet agreed to perform but I'm con-
            fident he will. Today, with your permission, I'll be reading
            his lines. Are we ready? Shall we form our circle? Mr.
            Carney, will you do us the honor?

CARNEY: Let us pray.

            SAINT IMELDA,
            SMILE ON OUR FIRST REHEARSAL DAY.
            BLESS THIS HUMBLE SEMI-PROFESSIONAL PLAY!

ALL: SAINT IMELDA
            HELP US CREATE A THING OF ART.
            AS WE START OUR FIRST
            REHEARSAL . . .

ALFIE: Mr. William Shakespeare said it best. "O for a muse of fire,
            that would ascend/The brightest heaven of invention! A
            kingdom for a stage, princes to act,/And monarchs to
            behold the swelling scene." Language like that almost
            makes you think the man was Irish! When he spoke for his
            rounded O of a theatre, he spoke for all of us. What is the
            difference between the Globe and this church social hall?
            None. We are both infinite.

            FEEL THE MAGICAL RING SURROUND US
            TRANSFORMING US AS WE ARE
            FROM GIRL ON A BUS TO PRINCESS,
            A LIGHTBULB TO A STAR!
            IT'S AS IF WE WERE THREE OR FOUR YEARS OLD
            AT OUR FIRST PUNCH AND JUDY SHOW.
            ON THIS MAGICAL DAY
            WE ENTER OUR PLAY
            AND WHO KNOWS WHERE WE MAY GO.

ALL: WHO KNOWS WHERE WE MAY GO.

ALFIE: At rise. The terrace of Herod's palace. A bloody moon.

(THE ACTORS *begin to read through actual lines from top of play*)

TRANSITION

THE BUS DEPOT/GARAGE

(ROBBIE *is stripped to the waist as he works to put a tire on a rim.* ALFIE *is with him.*)

ROBBIE: Stop your nattering, man, and give us a hand.

(ALFIE *tries to help* ROBBIE *with his work*)

ALFIE: Why do you say "no" to something you've never tried?

ROBBIE: There's a lot of things I've never tried that I never intend to and play acting is one of them. Use some strength, man!

ALFIE: I am!

ROBBIE: So you can stop trying to get me in tights and a wig and spouting poetry! Your audience would be in stitches but no one would be laughing harder than me. Alfie, didn't you never get a look at me skinny legs when we was changing?

ALFIE: No one would be laughing, including you, if you spoke the words of a great writer from the heart. The tights, the wigs: that's the folderol of theatre. In the theatre, it's your heart we're after.

ROBBIE: Well my heart is set on getting to a pub. To hell with this tire. The rim's all bent. Carson can fix it himself. I got you all dirty. Come on, we'll put on a clean shirt and call it a day. Don't look so crushed. I'm not an actor. I don't know about your sort of stuff, art and all. I'm an ordinary bloke.

(*They will change into their civvies during this*)

ALFIE: You're not ordinary, Robbie.

ROBBIE: You just say that 'cause you like me. Come out with me and me mates some evening, you'll see how ordinary I am.

ALFIE: All of your scenes would be with Miss Rice, none with Mrs. Grace. Salome's the key. Miss Rice will be splendid. She's like a dove that has strayed.

ROBBIE: She acts innocent.

ALFIE: She is innocent. She is a virgin. She has never defiled herself. She has never abandoned herself to men like other goddesses.

ROBBIE: Jesus, is that what you think?

ALFIE: I do, I do.

ROBBIE: Then you're more innocent than she.

ALFIE: I thought you were interested in Miss Rice.

ROBBIE: Why would I be interested in Miss Rice?

ALFIE: She's young, she's beautiful, she's a girl.

ROBBIE: Well I'm not. There must be something wrong with me!

ALFIE: Who . . . who are you interested in?

ROBBIE: (*Good-natured teasing*) That's for me to know and you to find out.

ALFIE: I meant.

ROBBIE: I know what you meant. Stop trying to fix me up with a bird neither of us knows the first thing about. Come to think of it, I don't know much more about you. We work together but who are you? What do you do at night? Where do you go? What fires burn in your loins, Mr. Byrne?

ALFIE: St. Imelda's is my life. Putting on plays. Those are my friends.

ROBBIE: I'm talking about reality. Out there. It's a real world, Dublin is. You're coming with me tonight.

ALFIE: My sister will be waiting supper for me.

ROBBIE: You've been taking tickets too long.

ALFIE: She'll take my head off.

ROBBIE: It's time you opened your eyes, man.

   (ROBBIE *and* ALFIE *head for the pub, and we open onto*)

"THE STREETS OF DUBLIN"

ROBBIE: I DON'T WANT TO STAND
          ON A STAGE WITH A SWORD.
          I WENT TO THE PANTOMIME ONCE.
          I WAS BORED.
          I'M NOT A POETICAL SORT OF A PERSON LIKE YOU.

WHEN I NEED A POEM,
THE STREETS AND THE GUTTERS WILL DO.

THERE'S TOMMY FLANAGAN WHO LIGHTS THE GAS
  LAMPS—
A HUNDRED NINETY LAMPS IN PHOENIX PARK
  ALONE.
HE'S DONE IT DRUNK FOR OVER FIFTY-SEVEN YEARS
  IN DUBLIN!

AND DOWN ON HENRY STREET IS MAD JOHN
  MAHER—
OLD RAMBLIN' JOHNNY WITH A FACE LIKE
  HAMMERED MEAT,
BUT JOHNNY'S SINGIN' BRINGS A DUBLIN MAN TO
  TEARS . . .

I DON'T KNOW
THE WORDS TO TELL YOU HOW IT FEELS
OR HOW TO PUT IT IN A RHYME
BUT IF YOU COME WITH ME YOU'LL KNOW
HOW THE LAMPS IN THE PARK
LOOK LIKE GOD IN THE DARK
AS THEY GLOW
ON THE STREETS OF DUBLIN.

THE DEALERS HAWKIN' AND THE DOCKERS
  YELLIN',
THE BUSKERS BANGIN' AND THE RAGMEN RINGIN'
  BELLS,
AND THERE'S MAUREEN WHOSE DOOR IS ALWAYS
  OPEN FOR
ALL DUBLIN!

AND TONY KIELY WITH HIS RACING PIGEONS.
IT'S LIKE RELIGION HOW HE LIVES TO FLY THOSE
  BIRDS—

HE SWEARS THEY TRAVEL FOR A HUNDRED MILES
    OR MORE . . .

I DON'T KNOW
THE KIND OF WORDS THAT YOU MIGHT SAY
BUT I CAN PUT IT MY OWN WAY,
AND IF YOU COME WITH ME YOU'LL KNOW
THAT THOSE BIRDS ON THE WING
ARE A BEAUTIFUL THING
AS THEY BLOW
THROUGH THE STREETS OF DUBLIN.

(*And at once we are in a noisy, smoky Dublin pub*)

AND THERE'S MUSIC LIKE NOTHIN' YOU'VE HEARD,
IF YOU KNOW THE RIGHT JUKEBOX TO PLAY!
THERE ARE GLASSES TO RAISE IN THE PRAISE
OF SURVIVIN' THE DAY . . .

DOWN WHERE . . .
MISS KITTY FARRELLY IS POURIN' WHISKEY
AND FRANKIE DONAHUGHE IS LIGHTING HER
    CIGAR.
A SMOKEY DEN WHERE WORKIN' MEN DON'T
    BRING THE WIFE . . .

IT'S THE LAUGHTER OF FELLAS WITH STORIES TO
    TELL,

MEN WHO LOVE TO GET DRUNK AND RAISE TRUE
    FECKIN' HELL!

AH, YOU COME OUT WITH ME AND YOU'LL SEE
WHAT YOU'RE MISSIN' IN LIFE

ROBBIE:	GROUP #1:	GROUP #2:	GROUP #3:
ON THE STREETS OF DUBLIN			
	ON THE STREETS OF DUBLIN		
		ON THE STREETS OF DUBLIN	
			ON THE STREETS OF DUBLIN
ON THE STREETS OF DUBLIN			
	ON THE STREETS OF DUBLIN		
		ON THE STREETS OF DUBLIN	
			ON THE STREETS OF DUBLIN
ON THE STREETS OF DUBLIN			
	ON THE STREETS OF DUBLIN		
		ON THE STREETS OF DUBLIN	
			ON THE STREETS OF DUBLIN
ON THE STREETS OF DUBLIN			
	DUBLIN		
		DUBLIN	
			DUBLIN

(ROBBIE *is very popular and very much at home at the pub*)

ROBBIE: Ladies and Gentlemen: I have the pleasure of introducing my work partner, theatrical producer extraordinaire and general hell raiser, Mr. Alfie Byrne. Drinks on me. Don't take his money, Kitty.

(*The publican is* KITTY, *an attractive blonde in her forties*)

KITTY: He's a queer-looking tulip.

ROBBIE: He's all right. I'll take the usual. (*To* ALFIE) Kitty thinks you're weird. She's right, you are! What'll you have, mate?

ALFIE: A Virgin Mary, please.

KITTY: I can get you a Mary, luv, but I don't know if she's gonna be a virgin.

(Laughter from the patrons)

ROBBIE: Where do you think you are, Alf? The Ritz? This is a workingman's pub. You and me are workingmen. Now what do you want that they might serve in a workingman's pub?

ALFIE: I'll have a pint.

ROBBIE: That's more like. A pint for my mate, Kitty. Come meet me mates.

(They join ROBBIE*'s friends who are shooting billiards)*

ALFIE: Hello.

ROBBIE: Alfie is me conductor. We're the Holy Terrors of the Dublin Transit System. I told you about him.

MATE #1:   The one who likes the theatre. Good a place as any to pick up a bird.

MATE #2:   You gonna sing something for us, mate?

ALFIE: What?

MATE #2:   We all sing here. We're Irish, we're drunk, what else are we gonna do?

ROBBIE: Cheer up, Alfie. It's only a song they're wanting. Singing is a window to a man's soul. Give 'em a look. It's sort of a ritual here. We all have to do it.

ALFIE: I'll do my best. I'm not really a . . . There is one I like.

"LOVE'S NEVER LOST"

ALFIE: IT WAS ON A MISTY SUNDAY
WE SAID OUR GOODBYE
AND I STILL CAN SEE HER SMILING,
A TEAR IN HER EYE.
SHE SAID "SON, PLEASE REMEMBER,
NO MATTER THE COST
YOU MAY TRAVEL FAR,
BUT LOVE'S NEVER LOST."
SO I TRAVELED DOWN THE HIGHROAD
AND FAR FROM TRALEE

(*This is met with much hostility and derision by the patrons*)

MATE #3:   What kind of Irish shite is that?

MATE #2:   I thought John McCormack was dead.

ROBBIE: Good try, Alfie. Wrong century that's all!

MATE #1:   Robbie, you in this round or not?

(ROBBIE *and his* MATES *take up cue sticks and prepare to shoot pool.* ALFIE *is suddenly alone in the pub.*)

KITTY: They're only having fun with you, luv. Boys will be boys. Give 'em time: their hearts will ripen. Jesus, that's an awful shake you have there, mister. Would you like a Woodbine to steady your nerves?

ALFIE: No thanks.

KITTY: I find them very soothing. Very handsome young chap that, your Robbie Faye.

ALFIE: Yes, very.

KITTY: More's the pity then.

ALFIE: What is?

KITTY: Someone like him getting involved with someone like that. It won't come to a good end. How can it?

ALFIE: I don't understand.

KITTY: I thought you were his mate. You and your big mouth, Kitty Farrelly!

(BRETON BERET, *a bad sort, has sidled up to* ALFIE)

BRETON BERET:
I liked your song, mate. You're a regular nightingale.

ALFIE: You're the only one who did.

BRETON BERET:
I like the old stuff. Very warm, it is, very dear. What's your name?

ALFIE: Alfie. Alfie Byrne.

BRETON BERET:
They call me Breton Beret for me headgear. So? What's up, Alfie Byrne?

ALFIE: Up? Nothing's up.

BRETON BERET:
I saw you looking at me.

ALFIE: I wasn't looking at you.

BRETON BERET:
       You were, Alfie. I was looking at you and you were definite-
       ly looking at me.

ALFIE: I have to go. My sister will be waiting dinner. Tell Robbie I'll
       see him tomorrow.

(*He starts to hurry away*)

BRETON BERET:
       I'm here every night, Alfie Byrne.

TRANSITION

LILY AND ALFIE'S APARTMENT

(LILY *is with* CARNEY. *They have been drinking.* CARNEY *paces
with the script of* Salome *in his hand;* LILY *is appalled at what she
is hearing.*)

CARNEY: This is filth, unadulterated pornographic filth. Just listen to
       this. Are you ready? Close your ears. (*He reads*) "I was a vir-
       gin and thou didst take my virginity from me. I was chaste,
       and thou didst fill my veins with fire."

LILY: Mr. Carney, I may have to ask you to leave, sir.

CARNEY: It's not me, Lil, it's his play. Wait, it gets worse. (*He looks for
       another offensive passage*) "Thou wert beautiful, Jokanaan.
       Thy body was a column of ivory. There was nothing in the
       world so white as thy body."

LILY: Is she talking about you, Mr. Carney?

CARNEY: Of course not, woman, I'm Herod. This is a sixteen-year
       old girl speaking to John the Baptist who was the first

Roman Catholic priest practically. And if that weren't bad enough, these words are spoken to a dead papier-mâché head.

LILY: I've stopped breathing. Here, this will steady our nerves.

(*She pours them each a sweet cordial*)

CARNEY: You know, Lily, I didn't realize until now what you've been put through by that brother of yours.

LILY: Oh, he was very strange from a child. A solitary boy, you know?

CARNEY: I'm not surprised.

LILY: Always off by himself, doing something strange. Puppets, he liked.

CARNEY: Puppets! What kind? Hand puppets or marionettes?

LILY: Both. He made them with his own little fingers.

CARNEY: Oh, Lily!

LILY: That room of his—it's always locked.

CARNEY: There'd be no locks if it was me. You must always have access. Without access you get salaciousness.

LILY: Do you know what's in his room? Books. Hundreds of books under lock and key.

CARNEY: Well there it is!

LILY: Mind you, he told me that they're all about railway trains.

CARNEY: I doubt it, Lily.

(*During the following song, the pouring and consuming of raspber-ry cordial continues*)

"BOOKS"

CARNEY: BOOKS.
THEY'RE AT THE ROOT OF IT.
BOOKS.
YOU KNOW, THEY'RE DANGEROUS—
ALL THAT JUNK PILED UP IN YOUR FLAT!

(*He tops up* LILY's *glass*)

HERE. HAVE SOME MORE.

LILY: (*Accepting*)
NOT ONLY THAT,
HE ...
COOKS!
REVOLTING FOREIGN THINGS.

CARNEY: COOKS!

LILY: CAN YOU IMAGINE IT!
PLATES OF STUFF WITH PARSLEY ON TOP!
HERE. LET ME POUR.

CARNEY: I'LL HAVE A DROP.

BOTH: BUT BOOKS!

CARNEY: IT ISN'T NATURAL!

BOTH: JUST THINK HOW BAD IT LOOKS
            TO PEEK THROUGH THE CRACK
            AND MEET WITH A STACK
            OF BOOKS!

LILY: He changes the locks continuously. He does it to thwart me.

CARNEY: We should attempt to keep him out of harm's way.

LILY: But you don't mean like St. James's hospital, do you?

CARNEY: No, Lily, I didn't mean to have him committed, but that's a
            fairly good idea. No, I was talking about marriage, Lily, my
            dear.

LILY: By rights, Mr. Carney, Alfie should be married and out of
            the house.

CARNEY: My sentiments exactly. And then, it will just be us, Mr. and
            Mrs. William Carney. Ah, Lily. I wouldn't stay out of the
            house.

            IF IT WAS ME
            I'D BE HOME AT FIVE
            WITH SOME CHOPS OR LIVER OR HAM.
            AND EVERY SINGLE SUNDAY
            WE'D HAVE LAMB.

LILY: Lamb.

CARNEY: WE'D TAKE A STROLL
            WATCHING PEOPLE PASS
            AND AT MASS, WE'D SHARE THE SAME PEW.
            OH, THAT'S WHAT I'D LIKE TO DO,

            Lily . . .

LILY: DON'T LOSE YOUR HEAD
            NOT TILL HE'S WED . . .

(ALFIE *enters, visibly shaken from his episode in the pub*)

LILY: Where have you been? I waited supper.

ALFIE: I went to the pub with a mate. I'm not hungry.

LILY: That lovely boiled cabbage you like.

ALFIE: I said I'm not hungry.

(*He goes into his room and closes the door*)

LILY: SOME DAYS
            I WONDER WHERE HE GOT
            SUCH QUEER AND FOREIGN WAYS.

CARNEY: HE GOT IT FROM ALL
            THE SMUT THAT HE READS.
            YOU KNOW WHERE SMUT
            EVENTUALLY LEADS!

LILY: HIS MANLY IMPULSES
            ALL BOTTLED UP!

CARNEY: WELL, THAT'S WHY
            THE POOR SOD COOKS!

BOTH: THE MAN NEEDS A WIFE
            TO RUIN HIS LIFE
            NOT BOOKS!

            Books!

Roger Rees as Alfie and Faith Prince as his sister, Lily. All photos from the 2002 Lincoln Center production of *A Man of No Importance*. Photo credit: Paul Kolnik.

Roger Rees as Alfie and Sally Murphy as Adele, his reluctant Princess
Salome. Photo credit: Paul Kolnik.

Roger Rees as Alfie and Steven Pasquale as Robbie, his bus driver and "Bosie."

Photo credit: Paul Kolnik.

Roger Rees as Alfie and Charles Keating as Oscar Wilde.
Photo credit: Paul Kolnik.

TRANSITION

ALFIE'S BEDROOM

(ALFIE *sits looking at himself in his bedroom dresser mirror*)

ALFIE: You've come to a pretty pass, Alfie Byrne. Take a good look at yourself, if you dare. Why would someone care for you when you care so little for yourself!

"MAN IN THE MIRROR"

ALFIE: MAN IN THE MIRROR
STARING BACK,
YOU'RE AS GOOD AS A TOTAL STRANGER.
HAIR GETTING THIN
AND CHIN GONE SLACK,
AN ANONYMOUS LITTLE MAN.
OSCAR WILDE HAD A BITING WIT:

"One should always be in love. That's the reason one should never marry."

AND A POET'S HEART.

"O Singer of Persephone! In the dim meadows desolate, dost thou remember Sicily?"

What is my wit? My poetry? "Change here for the Malmut Street Line! Have your fares ready! Next stop Nightingale!" That's not it, Alfie. Be honest. Look, it's in the eyes. The dead eyes of a man who does not know who he is.

HERE IN THE MIRROR
EVERY NIGHT
IS THE FACE OF A MAN IN PRISON.

> OSCAR, YOU BURNED
> SO BRAVE AND BRIGHT
> BUT THERE'S SOME OF US NEVER CAN.
> THERE'S SOME OF US NEVER CAN.

(OSCAR WILDE, *played by* CARNEY, *comes forward*)

ALFIE: Oscar Fingal O'Flahertie Wills Wilde. You wouldn't have noticed me either.

OSCAR WILDE:
"There is no hell but this, Alfie Byrne, a body without a soul; or a soul without a body."

ALFIE: I'm frightened.

OSCAR WILDE:
I know, I know.

ALFIE: WHERE IS MY GOLDEN LOVE?
WHERE BUT IN MUSTY PLAYS?
WHO IS THIS MAN IN THE THICKENING BODY
RIDING A BUS
TO THE END OF HIS DAYS ...

OSCAR WILDE:
"Sins of the flesh are nothing. Sins of the soul alone are shameful."

ALFIE: MAN IN THE MIRROR
STARING BACK,
YOU'RE AFRAID OF YOUR OWN REFLECTION.
ALL THAT YOU WANT
AND DREAM ... AND LACK
AND THERE'S NO ONE BUT YOU TO BLAME.
AFRAID OF THE WORLD,
AFRAID OF MYSELF

AND THE LOVE THAT DARE NOT SPEAK
ITS NAME . . .

OSCAR WILDE:
    AND THAT NAME IS . . .

ALFIE: Robbie.

TRANSITION

ST. IMELDA'S HALL

(*A rehearsal is in progress. Everyone is present but* CARNEY. ALFIE
is working with ERNIE *while the others practice words and gestures
among themselves.*)

MISS CROWE:
    My dear, may I make a suggestion? When you're speaking
    to me, always be sure to face away from the audience. That's
    right, your back to them. It's called upstaging.

ADELE: Thank you, Miss Crowe.

MISS CROWE:
    Just little tricks of the actor's craft, my dear. You'll catch on.

ADELE: My instinct is to face front.

MISS CROWE:
    (*Motherly*) I know, it's a common error beginners make.

MRS. CURTIN:
    (*Projecting*) Can you hear me, Mr. Byrne?

ALFIE: Perfectly, Mrs. Curtin.

MRS. CURTIN:
> (*Dramatically lower*) Can you still hear me?

ALFIE: Yes! Please, we're rehearsing.

MRS. CURTIN:
> I have a famous stage whisper, Miss Rice. Took me years.

MRS. GRACE:
> She's a little old for me daughter, Mr. Byrne. Could she be me sister?

ALFIE: Out of the question, Mrs. Grace. Again, Mr. Lally.

ERNIE: "You must not look at her. You look too much at her."

ALFIE: Mr. Lally, would you mind if we did it just once more?

MRS. GRACE:
> When do we get our John the Baptist?

ALFIE: Soon, Mrs. Grace. Now silence, all of you. Not a pin. We're working here. Again, Mr. Lally. (*Giving him his cue*) "How pale the princess is. Never have I seen her so pale. She is like the shadow of a white rose in a mirror of silver."

ERNIE: "You must not look at her. You look too much at her."

ALFIE: Um, Mr. Lally, a moment. (*He takes* LALLY *aside*) This is art, Mr. Lally, you understand, art. And art never expresses anything but itself.

ERNIE: What does that mean, Mr. Byrne?

ALFIE: It means . . . quieter, Mr. Lally. Try it once more. "She is like the shadow of a white rose in a mirror of silver."

ERNIE: "You must not look at her. You look too much at her."

ALFIE: Better. Better. Much better. I believe that's as much as we
            can do this evening without our Herod.

ERNIE: You were very good as Herod tonight, Mr. Byrne.

ALFIE: Thank you, Mr. Lally, but that's not the point.

ERNIE: Mr. Carney spits when he acts. Last play he got me all wet.

MRS. GRACE:
            I certainly hope Mr. Carney will favor us with his presence.
            I cannot rehearse my scenes alone.

ALFIE: When an artist like Mr. William Carney is unable to assist
            at rehearsal, I'm sure it's for a very good reason, Mrs. Grace.
            I will see you all tomorrow evening at seven. Good evening,
            my dear friends.

ALL: Good evening, Mr. Byrne.

   (LILY *enters, making sure* ALFIE *doesn't see her*)

LILY: Excuse me—are you Miss Rice?

ADELE: I am.

LILY: I'm Mr. Byrne's sister, Lily. I knew it was you right away.

           "THE BURDEN OF LIFE" (REPRISE)

LILY: MY BROTHER WAS TELLING THE TRUTH
            WHEN HE SAID
            THAT A PRINCESS GOT ONTO HIS BUS.

HE'S TALKED ABOUT GIRLS IN THE PAST NOW AND
    THEN,
BUT HE'S NEVER MADE QUITE SUCH A FUSS.
HE BAKED YOU HIS OWN SPECIAL SCONES
AS A TREAT.

IF ONLY YOU KNEW HOW HE TOILED!
THAT BOARDINGHOUSE FOOD MUST BE AWFUL TO
    EAT.
BUT HIS COOKING COULD GET A GIRL SPOILED.
OH! THERE'S SOME EGGS IN THE BAG,
WHICH I BOILED.

ADELE: I'm not much of a cook either, Mrs. . . .

LILY: Miss. That's something else we have in common.

ADELE: What's the other?

LILY: My brother.

LILY: NOW, ALFIE IS CRIPPLED WITH SHYNESS, AND SO
    INVITATIONS ARE ALL UP TO ME.
    AND HEARING HIM TALK ABOUT YOU I JUST KNEW
    HE WOULD LOVE TO INVITE YOU FOR TEA.
    IT'S SAD WHEN A FELLA SO DECENT AND NICE
    HAS SPENT HALF HIS LIFE ON THE WING.
    LET'S MAKE IT FOR DINNER THIS SUNDAY, MISS
        RICE.
    AND I PROMISE I WON'T COOK A THING.

ALFIE: Lily, what are you doing here? Where's Mr. Carney?

LILY: It's his Sodality night, he's the secretary, you know that. I'm just telling Miss Rice what a bang-up cook you are. We'll put some meat on your bones, dear. No one likes a skinny Salome.

ALFIE: Don't mind my sister, Miss Rice.

ADELE: Well, I'm off.

LILY: Alone? At this time of night? You're not in the country anymore, Miss Rice. You're a single girl in Dublin. Anything could happen, believe me. My brother will walk you home.

ADELE: Really, I'm fine.

ALFIE: What about you, Lil?

LILY: I'm waiting for Mr. Carney. I'm fine. Go on.

ALFIE: All right, Miss. Rice. We can talk about the play.

LILY: Forget the play, for once. I'm sure Miss Rice has other things she would like to talk about. Sunday dinner then, Miss Rice!

(ALFIE *and* ADELE *leave* LILY *alone in the theatre*)

THIS SAFE LITTLE WORLD
WHERE HE LIVES IN HIS FANCIES
AS IF HE WERE STILL EIGHT OR NINE.
IT'S TIME TO GROW UP, ALF.
IT'S TIME TO STEP OUT.
AS FOR FANCIES,
IT'S TIME I HAD MINE.

SHE'S YOUNG AND SHE'S PRETTY
AND READY TO DANCE.
AND THERE IN HER EYES I COULD SEE
A HOPEFUL YOUNG THING
ON THE BRINK OF HER CHANCE
VERY MUCH LIKE THE GIRL THAT WAS ME.
GOD SENT YOU THIS GIRL.

ALFIE, GIVE IT A WHIRL.
FOR THE SAKE OF THE GIRL THAT WAS ME.

TRANSITION

PHOENIX PARK

(ALFIE *and* ADELE *are strolling. There are other couples, lovers, walking in the park.*)

ADELE: You don't really want to, do you?

ALFIE: I'm sorry, I'm on another planet when I'm rehearsing a play. What?

ADELE: Go out with me.

ALFIE: Of course I do. I enjoy your company.

ADELE: No, no, I mean, *step* out with me. Like your sister said. She's trying to fix us up.

ALFIE: I know.

ADELE: Listen, Mr. Byrne, there's something I wanted to tell you but I never got the chance.

ALFIE: You have a boy. You have a fella.

ADELE: Yes. You see, you know very little about me really. I think you think more of me than I deserve.

ALFIE: You seem to me perfect, Adele. And your young fella: are you fond of him?

ADELE: Yes.

ALFIE: Ah! Young love is a lovely thing. Or so I'm told. And is he here in Dublin?

ADELE: No.

ALFIE: And what's he called, this lucky young man who's loved by a princess?

ADELE: John.

ALFIE: That's a coincidence. Just like our play. He's a very lucky fella, this John of yours.

(ADELE *suddenly gets tearful. Surprised,* ALFIE *gives her a hand-kerchief*)

ADELE: It's all right. I'm just being stupid. People are very harsh judges you know.

ALFIE: Why should anyone judge you, my princess?

ADELE: Oh, I'm far from a princess, far from it. But I know you won't judge me too harshly.

ALFIE: Who is anyone to judge you?

"LOVE WHO YOU LOVE"

ALFIE: I'M NOT ONE TO LECTURE.
HOW COULD I DARE?
SOMEONE LIKE ME
WHO'S BEEN MAINLY NOWHERE.
BUT, IN MY EXPERIENCE,
BE AS IT MAY,
YOU JUST HAVE TO LOVE
WHO YOU LOVE.

YOU JUST HAVE TO LOVE
WHO YOU LOVE.

YOUR COMMON SENSE TELLS YOU
BEST NOT BEGIN,
BUT YOUR FOOL HEART
CANNOT HELP PLUNGIN' IN,
AND NOTHING AND NO ONE
CAN STAND IN YOUR WAY.
YOU JUST HAVE TO LOVE
WHO YOU LOVE.
YOU JUST HAVE TO LOVE
WHO YOU LOVE.

PEOPLE CAN BE HARD SOMETIMES,
AND THEIR WORDS CAN CUT SO DEEP.
CHOOSE THE ONE YOU CHOOSE, LOVE,
AND DON'T LOSE A MOMENT'S SLEEP.
WHO CAN TELL YOU WHO TO WANT?
WHO CAN TELL YOU
WHAT YOU WERE DESTINED TO BE?
TAKE IT FROM ME . . .

THERE'S NO FAULT IN LOVING.
NO CALL FOR SHAME.
EVERYONE'S HEART
DOES EXACTLY THE SAME.
AND ONCE YOU BELIEVE THAT,
YOU'LL LEARN HOW TO SAY:
I LOVE WHO I LOVE
WHO I LOVE.
THEN JUST GO AND LOVE
WHO YOU LOVE.

ADELE: Here's where I'm staying. I'd invite you in, but I only have
one room and they don't allow guests.

ALFIE: I understand.

ADELE: Thank you for walking me home.

ALFIE: My pleasure entirely, Miss Rice. Adele.

ADELE: You're very nice. Mr. Byrne, I hope you're not cross about John.

ALFIE: No, no. That's a source of joy to me. To know that you love someone and that they love you in return. Adele, the love that dare not speak its name, do you know what that is?

ADELE: I don't, Mr. Byrne, to be honest.

ALFIE: Till tomorrow, Princess Salome.

ADELE: Till tomorrow, Mr. Byrne.

TRANSITION

THE STREET

(*We follow* ALFIE *as he begins his solitary walk home. He is very aware of his loneliness.*

Suddenly, out of the shadows steps the BRETON BERET.)

BRETON BERET:
          It's the nightingale. You got another tune for us, luv? No? Then how about a cigarette?

ALFIE: Sorry, I don't smoke.

BRETON BERET:
          Neither do I. Filthy habit.

ALFIE: I don't understand.

BRETON BERET:

Oh, I think you do, Alfie Byrne! (ALFIE *hurries on*) What's your hurry, man? The night is young and so am I. You know where to find me!

(BRETON BERET *disappears in the shadows as quickly as he appeared.*

ALFIE *stands for an undecided moment.* OSCAR WILDE *appears.*)

OSCAR WILDE:

The only way to get rid of temptation is to yield to it.

(*The sounds of Dublin rise as lights dim on* ALFIE)

END OF ACT I

 # ACT II

(*Lights come up on the members of a pub band, who play a vigorous melody. One of them is* ROBBIE. *In counterpoint, we see* MRS. PATRICK *singing a hymn. The action alternates between them, until they all merge, musically.*)

MRS. PATRICK:

    OUR FATHER, BLESS OUR HEARTS.
    OUR FATHER, GRANT US GRACE.
    OUR FATHER, CLEANSE OUR SINS.
    OUR FATHER, SHOW THY FACE.

(ROBBIE'*s band plays again. And now they join, and play and sing together.*)

    OUR FATHER, GUIDE OUR WAY.
    OUR FATHER, SET US FREE.
    OUR FATHER, MAKE US PURE.
    OUR FATHER, BLESS-ED BE.

MRS. PATRICK (AND CHURCHGOERS):

    FOR YOU ARE THE POW'R AND THE GLORY,
    YOU ARE THE LIGHT AND THE WORD.
    YOU ARE THE STRENGTH IN OUR STORY.
    YOU ARE THE SWORD.

    AMEN.

(ALFIE *is kneeling on one side of a confessional as* FATHER KENNY *listens on the other*)

ALFIE: Bless me, Father, for I have sinned. It's been a week since my last confession.

FR. KENNY:
A good sinner can get into a lot of mischief in a week. I'm listening.

ALFIE:
I SWORE AT MY SISTER
ONCE OR TWICE.
SAID SOME PRETTY BAD WORDS,
I S'POSE.

FR. KENNY:
Is that all?

ALFIE: AND I THOUGHT ABOUT KILLING
MY SUPERVISOR,
A NUMBER OF TIMES, GOD KNOWS.

FR. KENNY:
Now you're talking.

ALFIE: AND I SLEPT THROUGH YOUR SERMON.
SORRY, FATHER.
I DON'T KNOW WHERE I'VE BEEN,
THE WAY THAT MY MIND KEEPS WANDERING,
FATHER,
IT'S A SIN.

(ROBBIE *appears*)

ROBBIE: Dear Father, forgive this poor, lonely sinner, Alfie Byrne.

HE THINKS ABOUT ROBBIE
ALL THE TIME
AND THERE'S NOBODY HE CAN TELL.

ALFIE: I cheated the Dublin Bus Company by letting a girl ride for free.

ROBBIE: AND HE'S STRUGGLING WITH
HIS CATHOLIC GUILT AND
HE'S CERTAIN HE'S BOUND FOR HELL.

ALFIE: I led someone to believe he had a leading role, when really it's only a supporting one.

ROBBIE: AND HE FEELS LIKE HIS HEART
IS BURSTING, FATHER,
HOW CAN HIS LIFE BEGIN?
ANOTHER DAY'S
GOING BY HIM, FATHER.
IT'S A SIN . . .

ROBBIE AND ALFIE:
IT'S A SIN

ROBBIE: WHEN THERE'S MUSIC
LIKE NOTHING YOU'VE HEARD
IF YOU KNOW THE RIGHT JUKEBOX TO PLAY.
WHEN THERE'S GLASSES TO RAISE
IN THE PRAISE OF SURVIVING THE DAY . . .
BUT YOU'RE HERE IN THE DARK
IN A LITTLE BOX
WITH A FELLA WHO
MIGHT KNOW LESS THAN YOU.
THEN YOU'LL HURRY HOME

AND LOCK THE LOCKS.
ANOTHER BOX TO CLIMB INTO . . .

For God's sake, man, tell him and then we'll go have a pint.

FR. KENNY:
Is that all, my son?

ALFIE: THERE'S ONE OTHER THING
YOU OUGHT TO KNOW.
I'VE BEEN TRYING TO FIND THE WORDS.

FR. KENNY:
And what would that be?

ALFIE: I . . . Well, I . . . No.

THAT'S ALL I HAVE TO SAY.

FR. KENNY:
Say five Hail Marys, two Our Fathers, and next time don't
take so much time telling me the same old sins, Alfie Byrne.

TRANSITION

THE CEMETERY

(*People are leaving the service.* FATHER KENNY *greets the parish-
ioners as they file out the door.*)

MRS. GRACE:
Lovely service, Father.

FR. KENNY:
How's Mr. Grace?

MRS. GRACE:
> Poorly as ever, thanks. Thank God for our little play.

FR. KENNY:
> (*Uneasily*) Ah, yes, well. Are you sure you wouldn't rather be putting on last year's play? *The Importance of Being Earnest.*

MRS. GRACE:
> Once one has discovered high drama—tragedy, even, Father—there's no going back to comedy. Instead of tickling your funnybone, I'll be wringing your heart this time.

(*She goes.* CARNEY *and* LILY *are next in line to acknowledge* FATHER KENNY; ALFIE *is a step or two behind them.*)

CARNEY: A fine service, Father, a fine service, if I do say so myself. One feels cleansed.

LILY: Clean as a whistle, Father. Not like those poor sinners over in England.

CARNEY: What can you expect from a country that's still a monarchy? They need a good exorcism, the lot of them.

ALFIE: (*Aside*) Jesus!

CARNEY: That special meeting of the Sodality, Father?

FR. KENNY:
> It's all set.

ALFIE: You're not going to miss another rehearsal, Mr. Carney?

CARNEY: Sometimes a man has a bigger fish to fry than his own little kipper.

LILY: That sounds ominous.

CARNEY: Only to a sinner. Only to a sinner.

LILY: You coming, Alfie?

ALFIE: I want to pay my respects to our Da. (*He nods toward a gravestone*)

LILY: Well don't be long. I've got the Sunday roast in. He'll understand.

(*She and* CARNEY *go as* BALDY *approaches with flowers for his wife's gravesite*)

ALFIE: That's a lovely bouquet.

BALDY: White French tulips for my Mary's grave. They were her favorite. I wonder if she knows what they cost now. We'd have a terrible row. (BALDY *sets down his flowers. They sit on a bench together and look at her grave.*) That's gonna be us one day. Me before you, no doubt. Gives a man pause.

ALFIE: "If I can only produce one beautiful work of art,
           I shall be able to rob malice of its venom
           Cowardice of its sneer
           And pluck out the tongue of scorn
           By the roots."

BALDY: Something's up with you, Alfie Byrne. You gonna tell me what it is?

ALFIE: It's my play.

BALDY: If that's all it is, you'll be fine. You always are.

ALFIE: Do you ever get lonely, Baldy?

BALDY: Of course I do, Alfie. Since Mary passed away, God rest her, there's scarcely a day. A man needs a partner, a helpmate. That's why God made man and woman.

ALFIE: Your Mary, she was a big woman.

BALDY: Break a bag of ribs, she would. Nothing like it. That's the best thing about marriage.

ALFIE: Ah.

"THE CUDDLES MARY GAVE"

BALDY: SHE MADE THE SODA BREAD OF ANGELS
AND THE HOUSE WAS ALWAYS CLEAN.
AND THE WAY SHE PRESSED A COLLAR,
I LOOKED FIT TO MEET A QUEEN.
BUT IF EVER THERE'S ONE MEMORY I'D SAVE,
WELL, IT'S THE CUDDLES
MARY GAVE . . .

AH, SHE WAS WARMER THAN AN OVEN
IN THE MIDDLE OF JULY.
FIRST SHE'D LIFT ME LIKE A FEATHER,
THEN SHE'D CRUSH ME LIKE A FLY!
IT WAS WONDERFUL AND FRIGHTENING TO BRAVE
THOSE MASSIVE CUDDLES
MARY GAVE.

HOW SHE'D TALK AS WE'D WALK
DOWN THE ROAD ON AN EVENING,
THE NEIGHBORS ALL CALLING HELLO.
JUST A GREAT, STURDY GIRL
AND A SMALL, SKINNY FELLA
BUT WE WERE WELL-SUITED, YOU KNOW.
IT DOESN'T SEEM SO LONG AGO . . .

NOW, I'LL BE BUTTONING A SHIRT
OR IN THE MIDDLE OF A SHAVE,
OR ESPECIALLY PUTTIN' FLOWERS
ON THE HEADSTONE OF HER GRAVE

AND I'LL THINK:
I'VE HAD A FINE, CONTENTED LIFE,
HAVING HAD MY MARY FOR A WIFE ...
AND THE ONLY THING
I STILL CAN'T HELP BUT CRAVE
WELL, IT'S THE CUDDLES
MY MARY GAVE.

That's what you need, a woman to cuddle you. Stop your mooning around, set you to rights, your own Princess Salome.

(*The lights fade on them*)

TRANSITION

ST. IMELDA'S SOCIAL HALL

(*The place is a beehive of activity as everyone goes about his or her appointed tasks for the production of* Salome. ALFIE *is the one they all come to for approval.*)

ERNIE: Mr Byrne. I've been reading the script as the propmaster this time, not the Second Capodocian. I don't know which is more daunting.

"ART"

ERNIE:

> I WAS TOSSIN' ABOUT
> THE PROP DESCRIPTION
> WRITTEN ON SIXTY-FOUR,
> AND I WAS HOPIN' AS HOW
> I'D LIKE TO GIVE YOU
> SOMETHIN' A WEE BIT MORE.
> THIS IS ONLY A SKETCH.
> IT'S VERY ROUGH,
> BUT YOU SAID:
> "ART CAN'T GO FAR ENOUGH!"
> SO, THIS IS THE REAL STUFF!

(ERNIE *reveals a papier-mâché head on a plate*)

> I tried red paint first but it wasn't realistic. Then I tried real blood but it was too realistic. Don't want to frighten the audience. I think tomato catsup oughta do the trick if Miss Rice doesn't mind the smell. What do you think, Mr. Byrne?

ALFIE: What is it, Mr. Lally?

ERNIE: The head of John the Baptist.

ALFIE: I thought it might be.

ERNIE:

> IF YOU AREN'T CONTENT,
> THERE'S HEADS AND HEADS.
> I'LL TEAR THE WHOLE
> FECKIN' THING TO SHREDS!
> AND A WEEK AND A HALF FROM NOW
> THIS WILL BE ART!

(*Now* MISS CROWE, *the costume designer, approaches* ALFIE, *a tape measure around her neck, pins on her bodice, etc.*)

MISS CROWE:

> Mr. Byrne, those seven veils pose a great challenge to a designer, but I hope you'll think I've found a solution.

> I'VE BEEN FIGURING OUT
> SALOME'S COSTUME—
> ALL OF THE SMALL DETAILS.
> I'M TRYIN' TO FIND
> A NEW INTERPRETATION
> OF SEVEN VEILS.
> THIS IS JUST AN IDEA.
> BE HONEST, PLEASE!
> BUT YOU SAID:
> "ART USES WHAT IT SEES!"
> AND THEY'RE HAVING A SALE ON THESE.

(MISS CROWE *displays a dress dummy with seven veils, all hemmed with zippers*)

> Zippers. Seven zippers for seven veils. Zip, zip, zip, zip—

(ALFIE *interrupts her before she finishes*)

ALFIE: Stop! I don't think they had zippers in Biblical times, Miss Crowe.

MISS CROWE:

> (*Always the realist*)
> YES, THE ZIPPERS ARE TOO RISQUE, PERHAPS
> IN BIBLICAL TIMES,

> Did they have snaps?

> WELL, A WEEK AND A HALF FROM NOW
> THIS WILL BE ART!

(RASHER FLYNN, *the set designer, approaches with an electrical box*)

RASHER FLYNN:
> Mr. Byrne, look up there, please. I took the image of the moon as my chief inspiration.

> WELL, IT GAVE ME A THOUGHT
> FOR HOW TO GET
> THE SETS AND THE LIGHTS FOR FREE.
> YOU SEE, MY BROTHER-IN-LAW,
> THE ELECTRICIAN,
> OWES ME A THING OR THREE.
> SO HE GAVE IT SHOT.
> HERE'S WHAT HE MADE.
> 'CAUSE YOU SAID:
> "TRUE ART IS UNAFRAID!"
> AND HE WORKED WITHOUT BEIN' PAID!

(*The moon explodes*)

ALFIE:
> IT'S A COLLABORATION.
> THERE WILL BE FAILURES AND FRUSTRATION
> AND ALL THE TIME AND SWEAT AND TEARS
> YOU GIVE AWAY
> TO DO A PLAY . . .

MRS. GRACE:
> Mr. Byrne, I have the odious responsibility of bringing up publicity.

ALFIE:
> On the contrary, Mrs. Grace, we rely on you for a full house.

MRS. GRACE:
> In creating a poster for this production, I did not want to do the obvious. You know, an attractive young woman in a skimpy costume. My solution? The primal image of

Salome's mother, Herodias herself, earth mother, tigress, empress, woman.

ALFIE: You mean a picture of you?

MRS. GRACE:
That's a narrow way of looking at it, Mr. Byrne.

(MRS. CURTIN, *the choreographer, approaches, wearing some sort of leotard and a headband*)

MRS. CURTIN:
Mr. Byrne, this play is no piece of cake for a choreographer.

I'VE BEEN STRUGGLING WITH
SALOME'S DANCE—
HOW NOT TO OFFEND A SOUL.
I WANT TO CHOREOGRAPH
TO MAKE THE DANCE
GROW NATURALLY FROM THE ROLE.
THIS IS MERELY A THOUGHT,
IT MIGHT BE CRAP.
BUT YOU SAID:
"CONVENTION IS A TRAP!"
SO, I THOUGHT I MIGHT TRY . . . TAP!

(MRS. CURTIN *does a "Seven Veils" tap routine*)

FIVE! SIX! SEVEN! EIGHT!
OOH!
UH! UH!
VEIL NUMBER ONE!
OOH!
UH! UH!
VEIL NUMBER TWO!
VEIL NUMBER THREE!

VEIL NUMBER FOUR!
FIVE!
SIX!

ALFIE: Stop! No, Mrs. Curtin.

MRS. CURTIN:
No?

ALFIE: I'm afraid not.

MRS. CURTIN:
Yes, it probably is a bit "moderne."
And the tapping is hard for some to learn.

WELL, A WEEK AND A HALF FROM NOW,
THIS WILL BE ART!

ALFIE: IT'S A COLLABORATION
AND YOU'RE A PART OF THE CREATION.
AND SEVERAL HUNDRED GOOD IDEAS
MAY COME AND GO . . .

ALL: TO SERVE THE SHOW!
WHEN YOU'RE TALKIN' ABOUT
THIS THING CALLED ART
MAKIN' IT YOUR IDEAL,
THERE IS NOTHING THAT YOU
WILL NOT DO
TO FEEL WHAT IT MAKES YOU FEEL.
LET ANYONE DARE
TO WONDER WHY
FOR ART WE LIVE!
FOR ART WE DIE!
AND A WEEK AND HALF FROM NOW,
THE CURTAINS PART.
A WEEK AND A HALF

ERNIE: The head!!

MISS CROWE:
　　　　The veils!

RASHER: The lights!

MRS. CURTIN:
　　　　The dance!!

BALDY: The sets!

MRS. GRACE:
　　　　My face!

ALL: A WEEK AND HALF FROM NOW
　　　　THIS WILL BE ART!

ALFIE: Now let's pick up with the final scene. Miss Rice?

(ADELE, *dressed as Salome and holding a silver salver with a papier-mâché head of Jokanaan, resumes with her lines as Salome.*)

ADELE: "I was a virgin, and thou didst take my virginity from me. I was chaste, and thou didst fill my veins with fire . . . Ah! Ah! Wherefore didst thou not look at me? If thou hadst looked at me thou hadst loved me. Well I know that thou wouldst have loved me, and the mystery of love is greater than the mystery of death."

ALFIE: Excellent, Adele. We'll try it again with the full company.

ERNIE: Mr. Carney's telling people it's a dirty play, Mr. Byrne.

MRS. GRACE:
　　　　Mr. Carney's upset with the size of his part. I told him: There are no small parts, only small actors.

BALDY: No one will ever say that about you, Mrs. Grace.

ALFIE: (*Including the full company*) This is for all of us. This, what we do here, our play, is not real life. And that is Wilde's great achievement: to take the crude clay of real life and to transmute it into art. So, though Salome is a belly dancer, she's as pure as quicksilver is pure. Do you see? Wilde had no life aside from art, remember that. He lived in the realm of the aesthetic. He never descended into the sewer. Now let's rehearse. Second Cappadocians, quickly, quickly. First Nazarene! First Nazarene! Complete concentration now. No smoking or eating. Or gum chewing. This is a very difficult scene for Miss Rice. Silence!

(ADELE *takes up the silver salver and addresses the head*)

ADELE: "What shall I do now, Jokanaan? Neither the floods nor the great waters can quench me passion."

ALFIE: "My" passion, not "me" passion. "My." No matter, no matter. Go on, Miss Rice.

ADELE: (*Beginning to break down*) "I was a princess and thou didst scorn me. And thou didst scorn me."

(*She stops completely*)

ALFIE: (*Going to her*) Now, now, now. Take your time, Miss Rice. This is the whole climax of our play.

ADELE: "I was a princess . . . (*She starts to sob*) and thou didst scorn me. I was a virgin and thou didst take."

MRS. GRACE:
This is no good!

ALFIE: Silence!

ADELE: "I was a virgin and thou didst take my virginity from me."

(*Unable to continue, she flees the hall, still dressed in her costume*)

ALFIE: Oh, Lord! Continue rehearsing. Baldy, run lines, will you? I'll go find Miss Rice.

MRS. GRACE:
          I hope you find Mr. Carney and a John the Baptist while you're at it. I cannot rehearse by myself!

TRANSITION

OUTSIDE ST. IMELDA'S

(ADELE *is still crying when* ALFIE *comes up to her*)

ALFIE: It's my fault, Miss Rice. I've been too hard on you.

ADELE: It's not you, Mr. Byrne.

ALFIE: It's the part. Even the great Sarah Bernhardt had trouble with it. She . . .

ADELE: It's not the part either, Mr. Byrne. I'm not what you think I am. I'm not your virgin princess. I'm going to have a baby, Mr. Byrne

ALFIE: But you're not married.

ADELE: No, I'm not.

(*She hurries off.* ALFIE *doesn't follow.* FATHER KENNY *enters.*)

FR. KENNY:

Alfie, they want you in the Sodality room.

ALFIE: I'm still rehearsing, Father.

FR. KENNY:

It'll have to wait. Mr. Carney called a special meeting. It seems there's a bit of a crisis with your play.

TRANSITION

ST. IMELDA'S SODALITY MEETING

"A MAN OF NO IMPORTANCE" (REPRISE)

MRS. PATRICK:

IT'S A RAINY DUBLIN EVENING.
LAMPS ARE GOING ON.
BLACK UMBRELLAS PASSING.
PEOPLE COME AND GONE.

BRETON BERET, SULLY:

THE SKY IS THE COLOR
OF FACTORY SLATE.
BUT THERE ARE LIGHTS

SULLY:	BRETON BERET:	MRS. PATRICK:
THROUGH THE RECTORY GATE.		
	OOH ... OOH ...	
		OOH ...

(The St. Imelda's Sodality meeting is in progress.)

CARNEY: I felt it was my duty to tell the Sodality what you were up to, Alfie.

THERE'S SOMETHING AMISS
BENEATH OUR ROOF.
THE PENNY'S DROPPED.
THIS PLAY OF HIS
IS BLASPHEMY
AND MUST BE STOPPED!

ALFIE: Excuse me, Monsignor . . .

CARNEY: THESE ARE CONFUSING TIMES.
YOU READ IT IN THE NEWS.
YOU HEAR IT IN THE SONGS THEY PLAY.

ALFIE: May I speak?

CARNEY: AND IN CONFUSING TIMES
BELIEVING IS OUR STRENGTH.
WHAT ELSE IS THERE TO GUIDE OUR WAY?

THESE AGENTS OF CORRUPTION,
THIS DOCUMENT OF LUST.
THE CHURCH WILL STILL BE HERE
AFTER THEY'RE ALL DUST.

ALFIE: You're talking about a masterpiece of dramatic literature.

CARNEY: To a heathen atheist your play may be some kind of masterpiece. To a devout Catholic it is an affront to everything
our Lord Jesus Christ stretched out his arms and died for.

MONSIGNOR:
The play is canceled and St. Imelda's Players is barred from
further use of the hall. Next order of business.

CARNEY: I was thinking of your soul, Alfie, nothing else.

> IN THESE CONFUSING TIMES
> I CLEAVE TO WHAT I KNOW,
> A SERVANT OF THE SACRED LAMB.
> YOU HAD ONE FOOT IN HELL.
> I ONLY MEANT YOU WELL.
> LISTEN, ALFIE,
> YOU KNOW WHO I AM

ALFIE: I know who you are: Queensbury!

TRANSITION

MRS. PATRICK:
> OOH ...

BRETON BERET:
> NOW THE SOUNDS OF ACCUSATION
> ECHO DOWN THE LANE,

SULLY AND BRETON BERET:
> ECHO IN HIS HEART AND
> ECHO IN HIS BRAIN.

SULLY, BRETON BERET, MRS. PATRICK:
> THE MAN HURRIES ON
> UP A ROAD PAST THE PARK,
> COMES TO A DOOR

MRS. PATRICK:
> TURNS A KEY IN THE DARK.

SULLY, BRETON BERET, MRS. PATRICK:
> OOH ...
> OOH ...

TRANSITION

THE BUS DEPOT/GARAGE

(ALFIE *has reached the garage and turns on the lights. He discovers* ROBBIE *and* MRS. PATRICK *making love.*)

ROBBIE: Oh, shite!

MRS. PATRICK:

Hello to you, too, Mr. Byrne. I guess this beats anything in one of your plays. (*To* ALFIE) You've stopped breathing. It's not healthy, luv.

ALFIE: Mrs. Patrick! I had no idea.

MRS. PATRICK:

I believe that's the point of an extramarital affair, Mr. Byrne. Now you can have the Sodality crucify *me*.

ALFIE: Damn the Sodality!

ROBBIE: What are you doing here anyway?

MRS. PATRICK:

This was bound to happen, Robbie.

ROBBIE: I'm glad someone knows, Mary. It shouldn't be like this. I love her and I want to marry her. She thinks I'm daff.

MRS. PATRICK:

He is daff. I'm forty years old. I have three kids. He'll meet someone his own age and forget all about me

ROBBIE: I will not and will you kindly stop talking like I'm not here? I love you, damnit.

MRS. PATRICK:
Love! Lord, that word causes more trouble than it's worth. You're lucky you and it are strangers, Mr. Byrne. What time is it? I've got to be home before *Lawrence of Arabia* lets out. I'm very grateful for long films. I wish they made more of them. I'll see you, Robbie.

(*She quickly goes*)

ROBBIE: Why are you looking at me like that?

ALFIE: She's a married woman.

"LOVE WHO YOU LOVE" (ROBBIE'S REPRISE)

ROBBIE: ARE YOU GON'TO JUDGE ME, ALF?
TELL ME I'M A SORRY SIGHT?
ARE YOU GON'TO TO SAY THAT
CONFESSION WILL SET ME RIGHT?
I DON'T GIVE A FECK FOR THAT!
NO ONE'S GOING TO TELL ME
WHAT'S PROPER TO DO—
LEAST OF ALL YOU!
YOU LIVE WITH YOUR SISTER
AND DON'T GET OUT.
WELL, POEMS WON'T TEACH YOU
WHAT LIFE'S ABOUT,
OR HOW IT FEELS
LOVIN' SOMEONE WHO
CAN'T... WALK DOWN THE STREET WITH YOU!

This is my life. This is who I love. Love someone yourself before you judge me.

(*He goes*)

ALFIE: I do.

TRANSITION

ALFIE'S BEDROOM

(ALFIE *goes to his dressing table and begins to make up. The company crowds around him as he begins a transformation.*)

"MAN IN THE MIRROR" (REPRISE)

SULLY: SEE A DIMLY LIGHTED WINDOW
            FLICKER IN THE GLOOM.

BALDY: He parted his hair down the middle, Mr. Byrne. That's it!
            Straight down the middle.

MRS. GRACE:
            A dab of powder, a little rouge. Subtle, subtle!

BRETON BERET:
            LIFE AND ART CONVERGING
            IN A TINY ROOM . . .

MRS. CURTIN:
            Somebody get him a green carnation.

ERNIE: He never went out without a green carnation.

RASHER: It's how they know one another. It's their signal.

MRS. PATRICK:
            A MAN IN A MIRROR IS COMBING HIS HAIR,
            WATCHING HIMSELF AS HE STARTS TO PREPARE.

ROBBIE: (*Presenting* ALFIE *with a fresh green carnation*) Here you
            are, Mr. Byrne. Just came in down at the flower stalls, spe-
            cial for you.

ALFIE: Me darling boy. Ain't he a darling boy?

MRS. CURTIN:
        Oh yes. The darlingest boy we ever saw.

MISS CROWE:
        What's his name?

ALFIE: Bosie. Robbie.

ROBBIE, RASHER,
MISS CROWE, SULLY,
MRS. PATRICK:

WHERE IS MY
  GOLDEN LOVE?

WHERE BUT IN
  MUSTY PLAYS?

MRS.GRACE,
BRETON BERET,
ERNIE, MRS.CURTIN:

WHERE IS MY
  GOLDEN LOVE?

WHERE

GROUP 1:
  MAN IN THE
    MIRROR
  HERE YOU ARE
  MAN IN THE
    MIRROR
  HERE YOU ARE

  MAN IN THE
    MIRROR
  MAN IN THE
    MIRROR

GROUP 2:

MAN IN THE
  MIRROR
HERE YOU ARE

MAN IN THE
  MIRROR

MAN IN THE
  MIRROR

GROUP 3:

WHO CAN TELL
  YOU

WHO TO LOVE
WHO CAN TELL
  YOU

WHO TO BE
MAN IN THE
  MIRROR

(OSCAR WILDE *comes forward. He is carrying a set of "Oscar Wilde" regalia for* ALFIE: *broad-brimmed hat, evening cape and walking stick.*)

OSCAR WILDE:
　　　　One fiery-colored moment of great life! This is your moment, Alfred Byrne!

(*He puts the cape over* ALFIE'*s shoulders, sets the hat at the proper angle and hands him the walking stick.*

ALFIE'*s transformation is complete. He looks very much like Oscar Wilde.*)

ALFIE:　　Will you walk with me?

OSCAR WILDE:
　　　　But of course. I would consider it an honor.

(*The two Oscar Wildes begin their walk through the streets of Dublin*)

ALFIE:　　I couldn't have done this by myself.

OSCAR:　　Yes, you could. You are, in fact.

ALFIE:　　I feel . . . you'll laugh! I feel wonderful! Alfie Byrne is alive and walking the streets of Dublin with his good friend Oscar Fingal O'Flahertie Wills Wilde! I love to say your entire name.

OSCAR:　　Why? I never did. A name which is destined to be in everyone's mouth must not be too long. It becomes too expensive in the advertisements. See that house? I was born there. They put the plaque on the wrong house. (*Shakes his head*) You gotta love the Irish! (*Raucous sounds of a pub; they stop in front of it*) Well here we are. Go on. Don't be afraid.

ALFIE: You're not coming in?

OSCAR: MAN IN THE MIRROR,
STANDING HERE
WITH THE HOPE OF THE WORLD
BEFORE YOU.
DAMN THEIR DERISION. DO NOT FEAR
THESE ANONYMOUS LITTLE MEN.
ALFIE, YOU HAVE A BITING WIT!

ALFIE: "If one tells the truth, one is sure, sooner or later, to be found out."

OSCAR: AND A POET'S HEART.

ALFIE: "We have lived our lives in a land of dreams. How sad it seems."

OSCAR: The only way to get rid of temptation . . .

ALFIE: . . . is to yield to it.

OSCAR: Go.

TRANSITION

(ALFIE *goes into the pub.* OSCAR *disappears. All noise in the pub stops at the sight of* ALFIE. *The pub patrons part to reveal* BRETON BERET. *He almost seems to be waiting for* ALFIE. *They are in a direct line.*

Silence. ALFIE *walks directly up to* BRETON BERET *and whispers something to him.*)

BRETON BERET:
You want a what? A cuddle? A cuddle? Come on then.

(*He takes* ALFIE'*s hand and leads him out of the pub.*

As soon as they leave, the music in the pub is heard again and the PATRONS *resume their lively chatter and dart throwing.*

It is almost as if ALFIE *and* BRETON BERET *had never been there.)*

TRANSITION

ALLEY BEHIND THE PUB

(BRETON BERET *leads* ALFIE *to a dark place. They stop, facing each other.* BRETON BERET *removes* ALFIE*'s hat, loosens his scarf, then runs his finger through his hair.*

We are aware of other FIGURES *in the shadows.* ALFIE *isn't.*

BRETON BERET *pulls away a little and punches* ALFIE *in the face.*

ALFIE *goes down at once, soundlessly. The other* FIGURES *surge forward and begin to kick and pummel him.*

BRETON BERET *has already taken* ALFIE*'s wallet.)*

VOICE: Enough's enough.

VOICE: That'll do! That'll do, man!

ALFIE: (*Broken voice*) Bosie . . .

VOICE: What did he say?

VOICE: Bosie. He called you Bosie.

(POLICEMAN *blows a whistle*)

BRETON BERET: Fecking queer.

(*He throws* ALFIE'*s wallet at him. They are gone as quickly as they appeared as a* POLICEMAN *comes running down the alley.*)

POLICEMAN:
>All right, fella, come on. Who did this?

BYSTANDER:
>It's that lot from the pub. They're always beating up the queers.

ALFIE: There's only one thing for me now, absolute humility.

POLICEMAN:
>We'll see about that. Let's get you home first. You know where you live?

ALFIE: England. No, Paris. No. Ah yes, up there, in the stars. Take me up to the stars, officer, that's where I live.

POLICEMAN:
>Why do I always get the dozy ones!

(LILY *and* CARNEY *are seen walking together*)

CARNEY: Lily, you're a very clever woman. Could you tell me what a fondue is?

LILY: A fondue is a dog. Shiatsu, fondue, a Chinese dog. Why? Has somebody got one?

CARNEY: Mrs. Meehan was in the shop this morning and said she wants some meat for the fondue.

LILY: Free scraps she's looking for, for the little dog.

CARNEY: I knew I could rely on you.

(*They pass* ALFIE *and the* POLICEMAN)

LILY:　　God, isn't that Alfie? (*They surround him anxiously*) Jesus, Mary and Holy Saint Joseph, what's happened to your face?

ALFIE:　　I'm all right, I'm all right.

POLICEMAN:
　　　　　Do you know this man?

LILY:　　Know him? God, he's my brother.

CARNEY:　Of course we know him.

LILY:　　Look at that eye.

POLICEMAN:
　　　　　Well then, you take him home, please.

LILY:　　Alfie, who would have done this to you?

CARNEY:　What on earth's happened to him?

ALFIE:　　I did it to myself.

CARNEY:　Who were the perpetrators?

POLICEMAN:
　　　　　He's not gonna be pressing any charges. It's the usual thing. They never do.

CARNEY:　What are you talking about?

POLICEMAN:
　　　　　Look at him, man! He's a poofter!

(CARNEY *is thunderstruck at this revelation. He watches, dumbstruck, as* LILY *leads* ALFIE *home.*)

CARNEY: Am I the only who didn't know? How could I have been so stupid?

(*The other* ACTORS *look at one another*)

MRS. GRACE:
> I still don't believe it. Mr. Byrne is an artist. Artists are above that.

MRS. CURTIN:
> I am shaking. My nerves can't take such stress.

MISS CROWE:
> Our own Profumo Scandal rocking St. Imelda's to its foundations.

BALDY: Can we change the subject? This is not fit for public discussion.

ERNIE: It's public opinion we're talking about and this is a serious thing.

RASHER: I think we should all go home and say a prayer.

BALDY: That's the most intelligent thing that's been said all evening.

TRANSITION

LILY AND ALFIE'S APARTMENT

(*It is the next morning.* ALFIE *sits at the table with* LILY. *His face is bruised. One eye is swollen. There is a plate of food in front of each of them.*)

ALFIE: Eat.

LILY: I can't.

ALFIE: It's your favorite, sweetbreads.

LILY: When I think of where your hands have been!

ALFIE: That's the point—they've never been anywhere. They've never been close enough to anybody to rub up against them, let alone lay my hands on 'em. (*He has almost been shouting. Now he speaks with more control.*) The one person I like . . . well, love, damnit . . .

LILY: . . . is a fella.

ALFIE: Yes, Lily, it's a fella. But don't worry, because the very idea that I might love him, even feel special toward him, would be so repulsive to him that he wouldn't be able to get far enough away from me. So eat up. My hands are innocent of affection. Eat your breakfast.

"TELL ME WHY"

LILY: TO THINK THAT ALL THESE YEARS
           I NEVER EVEN KNEW YOU.
           WE SAT ACROSS THIS TABLE
           AND LIVED A LIE.
           HOW STUPID COULD I BE
           TO LOOK BUT NEVER SEE!
           NOW TELL ME WHY . . .

           I WASTED HALF MY LIFE
           AND PASSED UP ALL MY CHANCES.
           I THOUGHT I COULD PROTECT YOU.
           YOU LET ME TRY.
           HOW SELFISH AND HOW CRUEL

TO CAST ME AS YOUR FOOL!
AND TELL ME WHY

I STILL
DREAM ABOUT A DAY
I'M DANCING AT YOUR WEDDING.
I CATCH YOUR BRIDE'S BOUQUET
AND WAVE GOODBYE.
AND YOU, MY BABY BOY,
YOU'RE FIN'LLY ON YOUR WAY . . .
YOU'LL NEVER SEE THAT DAY.
AND ALFIE, NOR WILL I.

I SEE US
SITTING OUT OUR LIVES,
TWO PEOPLE AT A TABLE.
WE'RE LIKE A FADED PICTURE
IN SOME OLD FRAME.
YOU SHOULD HAVE TOLD ME, ALFIE.
WHY DID YOU NEVER TELL ME?

(ALFIE *leaves the room*)

YOU MUST HAVE KNOWN I'D LOVE YOU
ALL THE SAME.

TRANSITION

TROUPE MEMBERS:
IT'S ANOTHER DUBLIN MORNING.
'NOTHER DUBLIN SKY
NO ONE SAYS GOOD MORNING.
NO ONE WAVES GOODBYE.
A MAN FEELS THE CHILL AND IT CUTS LIKE A
KNIFE
AS HE HEADS OFF TOWARD THE REST OF HIS LIFE.

(ALFIE *arrives at his bus terminal, ready to work, as*
CARSON *enters*)

CARSON: The love that dare not speak its name, eh? Well it dared to
          speak its name last night by the looks of it.

ALFIE: I didn't speak love's name last night. That was me crime.

CARSON: You're lucky you're not in the prison.

ALFIE: I am in prison. I've been in prison all me life.

(THE NEW DRIVER *appears*)

NEW DRIVER:
          You Byrne? I'm your new driver. Keep your distance and
          we'll get on fine.

(*He takes* ROBBIE*'s chair, the driver's chair*)

ALFIE: Where's Robbie?

CARSON: Bosie, don't you mean? Well your Bosie's gone.

ALFIE: Me own boy.

CARSON: When I explained to your own boy the kind of man you
          are, and the things you do get up to, he was off like shot.
          Bang! Couldn't wait to get away from you. On your way
          now! The bus has a schedule whether you like it or not.

(*The bus is pulling away,* ALFIE *and* THE NEW DRIVER *ride at
opposite ends, all his friends palpably absent*)

TROUPE MEMBERS:
          PICTURE THE BUS
          AS IT MOVES DOWN THE STREET

PAST A WINDOW OF FISH
AND A PRIEST ON A BIKE . . .
TWO MEN ON A BUS
THAT COULD WELL BE A HEARSE,
EMPTY OF EVERY LAST ECHO OF VERSE . . .

ADELE: A BLUE-COATED GIRL,
WITH A SUITCASE IN HAND,
ENTERS THE BUS—
BUT SHE CHOOSES TO STAND.

ALFIE: Miss Rice!

ADELE: I came to say goodbye. I have to go to England.

ALFIE: To England?

ADELE: I need to go for me and the baby. He's moving already. Maybe he'll be a dancer like his mother.

ALFIE: And your feller, John, will he be going with you?

ADELE: He doesn't love me, Mr. Byrne.

ALFIE: But you're having his child. He must love you. You've been physically intimate.

ADELE: Oh, that isn't always love, you know. You're really innocent, aren't you?

ALFIE: I'm a man of the world, Miss Rice, just a man of the world!

ADELE: I was telling the truth, wasn't I? When I said I wasn't what you thought I was.

ALFIE: We've learned a horrible lesson.

ADELE: About me.

ALFIE: About myself.

"LOVE WHO YOU LOVE" (ADELE'S REPRISE)

ADELE: PEOPLE CAN BE HARD SOMETIMES,
          AND THEIR WORDS CAN CUT SO DEEP.
          CHOOSE THE ONE YOU CHOOSE, LOVE,
          AND DON'T LOSE A MOMENT'S SLEEP.
          WHO CAN TELL YOU WHO TO WANT?
          WHO CAN TELL YOU
          WHAT YOU WERE DESTINED TO BE?

          Oh, Mr. Byrne . . .

          THERE'S NO FAULT IN LOVING.
          NO CALL FOR SHAME.
          EVERYONE'S HEART
          DOES EXACTLY THE SAME.
          AND ONCE YOU BELIEVE THAT,
          YOU'LL LEARN HOW TO SAY:
          I LOVE WHO I LOVE
          WHO I LOVE . . .

    (*Then*)

          I'm sorry about your play. I'm sorry I couldn't be your
          Princess Salome. Goodbye, Mr. Byrne.

    (*She goes*)

BALDY: Curtain.

MRS. CURTIN:
          Your little dove has flown, Mr. Byrne.

MISS CROWE:
And so have we.

ALFIE: Your play has a sad ending.

MRS. GRACE:
Those who attempt tragedy must be prepared for an unhappy ending. Something like that.

ERNIE: Goodbye, Mr. Byrne.

(*They are all gone now*)

TRANSITION

ST. IMELDA'S SOCIAL HALL

(ALFIE *stands alone in the dull light of the empty rehearsal hall, looking at the rehearsal props, as in the first scene*)

"WELCOME TO THE WORLD"

ALFIE: YOU THOUGHT YOU KNEW A BIT OF LIFE
YOU HAD NO CLUE.
YOU TOOK A STEP, THE WORLD CAME CRASHING
DOWN ON YOU.
AND WHAT YOU FEARED THE MOST OF ALL
HAPPENED,
WELL, NOW YOU'VE COME TO . . .

WELCOME TO THE WORLD.
WELCOME TO THE WORLD AT LAST.
YOU'VE BEEN TAKING TICKETS
FAR TOO LONG, MY FRIEND,
WATCHING THE WORLD ROLLING PAST . . .

BUT THERE'S MUSIC LIKE NOTHING YOU'VE
        HEARD,
MR. BYRNE,
IF YOU JUST LET IT PLAY.
THERE ARE GLASSES TO RAISE
IN THE PRAISE
OF SURVIVING THE DAY

FOR LIFE IS CLEARLY SOMETHING
THAT I CAN'T REHEARSE

IT'S DANGEROUS AND BEAUTIFUL
AND FREE AS VERSE,
AND RATHER THAN AVOID IT,
IT'S HIGH TIME I STOOD IN ITS WAY . . .

WELCOME TO THE WORLD.
I AM IN THE WORLD.
THAT SHOULD BE ENOUGH
AND THAT'S ALL I HAVE TO SAY.

(*There is a shaft of sunlight as the outside door is opened. We cannot make out the figure standing there because of the bright backlighting.*)

ROBBIE: There you are.

ALFIE: Who's that?

(ROBBIE *turns on the overhead lights. His hair is an alarming blonde.*)

ROBBIE: I came to be in the play. Where's the actors?

ALFIE: What have you done to your hair?

ROBBIE: Do you like it?

(*He pulls off his wig and tosses it to* ALFIE)

ALFIE: I thought you'd gone. Left me.

ROBBIE: Don't mind that ol' shite Carson. He had me transferred but I'll be back.

ALFIE: Me own boy.

ROBBIE: None of that now. I know where you've been. I don't care what you get up to, I like you. You're me pal. And I know who Bosie was an' all. So where's this part you got for me in the play?

ALFIE: There is no play. They've all gone. Carney turned 'em all against me.

(BALDY *has come into the hall*)

BALDY: There's a chance we can use the hall at St. Dunon's. They're looking to do a *Heartbreak House*. I told 'em we got heartbreak a plenty.

ALFIE: Baldy! I thought you'd left me for good.

BALDY: And why would I do that, Mr. Byrne?

ALFIE: I'm a great sinner.

BALDY: You're a terrible director but we're staying.

(*He embraces* ALFIE *as the other* ACTORS *start crowding into the hall*)

MISS CROWE:
I don't know what you've done, Mr. Byrne, but I know you for a good man.

MRS. CURTIN:
     I never liked the acoustics in this hall.

ALFIE: Mrs. Grace, you of all people!

MRS. GRACE:
     (*Ignoring him*) I have a responsibility to art.

BALDY: Ah, stuff it, woman.

MRS. GRACE:
     I was speaking to Mr. Byrne. Life goes on and so must we
     artists.

ALFIE: I'm so blessed in my friends. Nothing else matters.

(LILY *enters with a silver salver filled with little sandwiches*)

LILY: Refreshments!

ALFIE: Carney provided the meats?

LILY: Are you daff? Of course not. I took them.

ALFIE: I've been wrong about something. I used to think the most
     thrilling words in the English language were "At Rise" as we
     began a new project and opened our books to the first page
     of the playwright's text.

MRS. GRACE:
     They still speak to me, Mr. Byrne.

ALFIE: No, Mrs. Grace, the most thrilling words in the English lan-
     guage are these: "Good morning, my dear friends."

ALL: Good morning, Mr. Byrne.

ALFIE: The future of our little troupe is uncertain but one thing is for sure: we have a new star in our theatrical firmament. I think you all know him.

(*They applaud for* ROBBIE)

ALFIE: Shall we form our little circle? Perhaps for the last time. (LILY *is about to excuse herself*) No, stay, Lil', you're welcome.

LILY: Well, don't get any ideas about me acting. I'm just doing the snacks.

(*She sits with folded arms*)

ALFIE: We have a tradition at St. Imelda's. The newcomer reads us a little something at his first appearance. It's not an audition, it's more like a rite of passage.

(*He hands* ROBBIE *a book*)

ROBBIE: It's that bleeding poetry again.

ALFIE: Read it.

(*The others lean in close as* ROBBIE *reads. After a while, even* PETER *will stop sweeping to listen.*)

ROBBIE: (*Haltingly, the meaning of the words sinking in*)
"Like two doomed ships that pass in storm,
We had crossed each other's way:
But we made no sign, we said no word,
We had no word to say.
For we did not meet in the holy night
But in the shameful day.
The prison wall was round us both,

(The lights are beginning to fade)

> Two outcast men we were:
> The world had thrust us from its heart,
> And God from out his care."

ALL EXCEPT ALFIE:
> A MAN OF NO IMPORTANCE.

THE END

TERRENCE MCNALLY was most recently represented on Broadway with the revival of his play *Frankie and Johnny in the Clair de Lune* and the book for the musical *The Full Monty*. He won his fourth Tony Award for Best Book of a Musical for *Ragtime* (music and lyrics by Stephen Flaherty and Lynn Ahrens). He is currently working on the book for *The Visit* with score by John Kander and Fred Ebb. McNally won the Tony in 1996 for his play *Master Class* in which Zoe Caldwell created the role of Maria Callas; the 1995 Tony, Drama Desk and Outer Critics Circle Awards for Best Play as well as the New York Drama Critics' Circle Award for Best American Play for *Love! Valour! Compassion!*; and the 1993 Tony for his book of the musical *Kiss of the Spiderwoman* (music and lyrics by Kander and Ebb). His other plays include *Corpus Christi*; *A Perfect Ganesh*; *Lips Together, Teeth Apart*; *The Lisbon Traviata*; and *It's Only a Play*, all of which began at the Manhattan Theatre Club. Earlier stage works include *Bad Habits, The Ritz, Where Has Tommy Flowers Gone?, Things That Go Bump in the Night, Next,* and the book for the musical *The Rink* (music and lyrics by Kander and Ebb). For the Central Park Opera trilogy presented at the New York City Opera in the fall of 1999 he wrote the libretto for *The Food of Love*, with music by Robert Beaser. The San Francisco Opera presented *Dead Man Walking* with McNally's libretto and music by Jake Heggie. McNally has written a number of TV scripts, including *Andre's Mother* for which he won an Emmy Award. He has received two Guggenheim Fellowships, a Rockefeller Grant, a Lucille Lortel Award, and a citation from the American Academy of Arts and Letters. He has been a member of the Dramatists Guild since 1970.

STEPHEN FLAHERTY has written music for theatre, film, and the concert hall. He won the 1998 Tony, Drama Desk, and Outer Critics Circle Awards for his score for the Broadway musical *Ragtime*. Mr. Flaherty also received Grammy Award nominations in 1998 and 1999 for the recordings *Songs from Ragtime* and *Ragtime: Original Broadway Cast Recording*. Other Broadway composing credits include *Seussical* (2001 Drama Desk nomination, 2002 Grammy Award nomination; also co-book writer and co-conceiver [with Lynn Ahrens and Eric Idle]), *Once On This Island* (1990 Tony nominations for Best Score and Best Musical; 1995 Olivier Award for London's Best Musical), *My Favorite Year* (Lincoln Center Theatre, 1992), and Neil Simon's *Proposals* (1997, incidental music). He is also the composer of the musical farce *Lucky Stiff* (Off-Broadway, 1988). All were written in collaboration with lyricist Lynn Ahrens. Film work includes *Anastasia* (1998 Academy Award nominations for Best Score and Best Song; two Golden Globe nominations). His concert pieces include "With Voices Raised" (text by Ms. Ahrens), a piece for large orchestra, chorus, tenor soloist, and speakers that was commissioned by the Boston Pops Orchestra and was subsequently performed at

Carnegie Hall, and "Ragtime Symphonic Suite" for orchestra. Both have been recorded by RCA Victor. Mr. Flaherty is a member of Drama Dept, ASCAP, and the Dramatists Guild, where he currently serves on Council.

LYNN AHRENS wrote lyrics for the Broadway musical *Ragtime* (based on the E. L. Doctorow novel), winning the 1998 Tony Award, Drama Desk Award, and Outer Critics Circle Award with collaborators Stephen Flaherty and Terrence McNally. She also received Grammy nominations for *Songs from Ragtime* and *Ragtime: Original Broadway Cast* recordings of the show. Also in 1998, she received two Academy Award nominations and two Golden Globe nominations for the songs and score of *Anastasia,* Twentieth Century Fox's first feature animation. Most recently Ms. Ahrens was represented on Broadway with book and lyrics for *Seussical* (Grammy nomination) and Off-Broadway with lyrics for *A Man of No Importance* (book by Terrence McNally, directed by Joe Mantello) at Lincoln Center Theatre. She wrote book and lyrics for the long-running Broadway musical *Once on This Island* (London's 1995 Olivier Award as Best Musical, eight Tony Award nominations, Drama Critics Circle, and Outer Critics Circle nominations); book and lyrics for *Lucky Stiff* (Playwrights Horizons; Richard Rodgers Award, Washington's 1990 Helen Hayes Award for Best Musical); lyrics for *My Favorite Year* (Lincoln Center Theatre). She was also commissioned by the Boston Pops Orchestra to write text for *With Voices Raised,* performed at Symphony Hall and Carnegie Hall. All the above have music by longtime collaborator Stephen Flaherty. Individually, Ms. Ahrens is the lyricist and co-book writer for *A Christmas Carol,* Madison Square Garden's annual holiday musical (music by Alan Menken, co-book by Mike Ockrent) now in its ninth year. For her work in network television as a songwriter, creator, and producer, Ms. Ahrens has received the Emmy Award and four Emmy nominations. Her songs are a mainstay of the renowned animated series *Schoolhouse Rock.* She is a member of ASCAP; the Academy of Motion Picture Arts and Sciences; Dramatists Guild Council; and on the Board of Directors, Young Playwrights Festival; she co-chairs the Dramatists Guild Musical Theatre Fellows Program.